SAGE was founded in 1965 by Sara Miller McCune to support the dissemination of usable knowledge by publishing innovative and high-quality research and teaching content. Today, we publish over 900 journals, including those of more than 400 learned societies, more than 800 new books per year, and a growing range of library products including archives, data, case studies, reports, and video. SAGE remains majority-owned by our founder, and after Sara's lifetime will become owned by a charitable trust that secures our continued independence.

Los Angeles | London | New Delhi | Singapore | Washington DC | Melbourne

ADVANCE PRAISE

'Mamta Chitnis Sen has captured the essence of what politics should be in talking about the functioning of grassroots politics. This has been done by examining the experiences and methods of politicians whose only *durbar* was the people. The analysis has been expertly woven together to create a work that is an essential reading for those interested in the roots of democracy in India.'

M. D. Nalapat, *UNESCO Peace Chair,*
Manipal Academy of Higher Education

'Mamta Chitnis Sen has boldly tackled the difficult subject of probing the motivation for any Indian to join the current-day Indian politics. What has happened to that pre-1947 confluence of ideologically inspired, freedom-seeking and educated individuals who are seldom seen now in any political party? Why has politics been converted into a power-seeking, sectarian and profit-based avocation?

The author highlights the reasons for this deterioration through the voices of grassroots workers from different political parties. Most of them spoke to her frankly, though one could discern attempts by some to shroud reality while facing the tape recorder. Some defended dynastic politics on public acceptability. Almost all of them spoke of difficulties in managing their professions while being in politics, which demanded full-time attention.'

Vappala Balachandran, *Columnist and Author*

'To be a successful political worker in any of India's several frontline parties is definitely a high order. It's like playing cricket in your 'gali' and aspiring to be the captain of the Indian team in a World Cup or a test series abroad! You have to work hard, very hard, and you can still be kept out of the playing XI. The ladder to the top is too steep.

Do the parties genuinely care for the unsung heroes working on the field? Does a party support the young dedicated workers who have no solid link with an established leader? Do youths have a future in political parties? Is there a good political training centre? How dirty is the political structure of our parties that claim to shoulder the responsibility of running a state or a country? Is there a career in politics? This book, to some extent, has tried to find answers to these inconvenient questions, and more.

Realpolitik attempts to expose the functioning of the parties from within. Since the author had had a stint at politics—even if at a junior level—she knows how the parties operate and what the future is for a young aspirant. This is a must-read for all the political greenhorns, as it shows them the trenches in the dark alleys much before they start to grope in and get badly bruised!'

Abhilash Khandekar, *Veteran Journalist and Political Analyst*

'A refreshing take on the inside world of politics, the book brings forth the actual workings of both the political parties and the people involved in at all levels. It is a must-read for those interested in pursuing a career in one of the most complicated fields in the world.'

Kripashankar Singh, *Ex-State Home Minister, Maharashtra, and Ex-President, Mumbai Regional Congress Committee (MRCC)*

'Mamta Chitnis Sen has spread her journalistic net to haul in a wide spectrum of political parties and personalities. It is an easy, well-written, well-researched guide through the maze of our contemporary polity.'

Mani Shankar Aiyar, *Ex-Union Minister, Panchayati Raj and Development of North Eastern Region, Youth Affairs & Sports*

'Mamta Chitnis Sen has attempted to decipher the complex world of politics lived and experienced by grassroots workers and their leaders. The book provides deep insights not only into the intricate workings of different political parties but also into the dynamics, importance and differing reasons for seeking power and the methods that one is forced to seek to achieve them. It is a must-read.'

Ashok Dhawale, *Central Committee Member, Communist Party of India (Marxist), National President, All India Kisan Sabha*

'Calculating the many reasons behind what makes Indian politics tick, Mamta Chitnis Sen has courageously ventured into navigating its tricky waters by bringing forth the reality and hard work that goes in not only running political parties in the country but also managing the many people associated with it. The book is surely an eye-opener and a guide for political first-timers.'

Sayyid Munavvar Ali Shihab Thangal, *President, Indian Union Muslim League*

REALPOLITIK

REALPOLITIK
EXPOSING INDIA'S POLITICAL SYSTEM

MAMTA CHITNIS SEN

Los Angeles | London | New Delhi
Singapore | Washington DC | Melbourne

Copyright © Mamta Chitnis Sen, 2020

All rights reserved. No part of this book may be reproduced or utilized in any form or by any means, electronic or mechanical, including photocopying, recording, or by any information storage or retrieval system, without permission in writing from the publisher.

First published in 2020 by

SAGE Publications India Pvt Ltd
B1/I-1 Mohan Cooperative Industrial Area
Mathura Road, New Delhi 110 044, India
www.sagepub.in

SAGE Publications Inc
2455 Teller Road
Thousand Oaks, California 91320, USA

SAGE Publications Ltd
1 Oliver's Yard, 55 City Road
London EC1Y 1SP, United Kingdom

SAGE Publications Asia-Pacific Pte Ltd
18 Cross Street #10-10/11/12
China Square Central
Singapore 048423

Published by Vivek Mehra for SAGE Publications India Pvt. Ltd. Typeset in 11.5/14.5 pt Arno Pro by Fidus Design Pvt. Ltd, Chandigarh.

Library of Congress Control Number: 2020942655

ISBN: 978-93-5388-544-1 (PB)

SAGE Team: Namarita Kathait, Shipra Pant and Kanika Mathur

To

My darling daughters, Toya and
Tonoya, for believing in me

My lifeline Sanjit for putting up
with my craziness

My rock Ratnakar for making
this book happen

Thank you for choosing a SAGE product!
If you have any comment, observation or feedback,
I would like to personally hear from you.

Please write to me at **contactceo@sagepub.in**

Vivek Mehra, Managing Director and CEO, SAGE India.

Bulk Sales

SAGE India offers special discounts
for purchase of books in bulk.
We also make available special imprints
and excerpts from our books on demand.

For orders and enquiries, write to us at

Marketing Department
SAGE Publications India Pvt Ltd
B1/I-1, Mohan Cooperative Industrial Area
Mathura Road, Post Bag 7
New Delhi 110044, India

E-mail us at **marketing@sagepub.in**

Subscribe to our mailing list
Write to **marketing@sagepub.in**

This book is also available as an e-book.

CONTENTS

Preface ix
Acknowledgements xiii

PART 1 MEASURE OF A POLITICAL PARTY 1
Chapter 1 Minions behind a Political Effigy 3
Chapter 2 Political Loyalty 21
Chapter 3 Ideological Cloning 35

PART 2 POLITICAL CAREER ROADMAP 49
Chapter 4 The Life of a Political Worker 51
Chapter 5 Political Godfathers and Dynasty Politics 71
Chapter 6 The Money Rota 83

PART 3 THE POLITICAL GAME OF THE MARGINALIZED 109
Chapter 7 Vote Bank Tokenism 111
Chapter 8 Women in Politics: Dodging Patriarchy 129

PART 4 OILING THE NUTS AND BOLTS 147
Chapter 9 Defections and Desertions 149
Chapter 10 Tickets and Appointments 167
Chapter 11 Political Leaderships 187

References 201
About the Author 203

PREFACE

My tenure as an office-bearer of the Youth Congress was a fascinating one. It not only provided me deep insight into the ways the machinery of a political party functions at all levels but the experience also provided me valuable education, both in my occupation as a political and a crime reporter in life. It also enabled me to understand and look at situations beyond mere optics—to decipher the reasons behind the decisions taken and their implications on others.

This book is not written to espouse one political ideology or favour any one party but to show the mechanism of the Indian political system and bring forth the reality that we do not live in an equal society but in an unequal one. While on the fringes all may seem fine, deep within, there is a constant struggle and churning taking place—an unrest, an invisible fight of the dominance of one's existence over another for wealth, position and eventually power.

Irrespective of their background, caste or creeds and social status, I came across many people (men and women) who sought power in some way or the other. While many desired to dominate over others, there were some who found solace in being dominated by those in power. I also discovered that politics is not restricted to political parties alone, but is present in every sphere of our lives— in our homes and offices; daily interactions with our family, friends and colleagues; and so on. Politics is very much ingrained in the Indian psyche and the ones aware of it utilize it to their maximum benefit, the ones who are not, are left behind in the rat race.

How much money does a party worker make? How much money do our political leaders spend on elections? What is the cost of contesting an election? Do political parties pay their leaders? This book raises these questions and includes interviews of party workers from key political parties and documents their journey, associations, road maps to making their respective parties victorious in elections, strategies, fundraising techniques, emotional investments, etc and eventually how these collaborations took a toll on their personal and professional lives.

Realpolitik: Exposing India's Political System is a tribute to their hard work and silent accomplishments behind the big political canvas and an insight into the stories that have never been told till date. The book also further examines the relationship between the grassroots workers and their party leadership, the fallouts that followed when they were ignored and eventually, how this feeling of disconnect and neglect translated into the decline in their party's political fortunes through election defeats.

This book explores, analyses and highlights the lives and experiences of political leaders, activists and all those associated with political parties in some way or the other and the sacrifices and the prices they paid along the way to uphold the ideology of their party or the cause. Managing a political party can be a tricky affair, but more complex and intriguing is the task of handling the many people associated with it. A glimpse into the lives of the many people who run and manage political parties only brings forth the harsh truth that politics is not about who is in power, politics is about who is controlling the person in power!

The book is divided into four parts, beginning with the life of the invisible party worker (the minions) to the mid-level functionaries, to the long-time loyalists and finally the leaders who control their 'kingdoms'.

I am thankful to the following political parties—Indian National Congress, Bharatiya Janata Party, Communist Party of India

(CPI), Communist Party of India (Marxist), Shiv Sena, Nationalist Congress Party (NCP), Indian Union Muslim League, the All Indian Majlis-e-Ittehad-ul-Muslimeen (AIMIM), Bahujan Samaj Party, Republican Party of India (RPI)—and its many factions, Samajwadi Party, All India Trinamool Congress (AITC), Maharashtra Navnirman Sena (MNS), Vanchit Bahujan Aghadi and Janata Dal (United) for agreeing to be part of this book and helping me reach out to their numerous followers and leaders.

I would also like to thank the following people for taking time out from their busy schedules to be interviewed for this book:

Mani Shankar Aiyar, Kripashankar Singh, Manohar Bothra, Nizamuddin Rayen, Nandita Hooda and Sushil Dalvi from the Congress; Madhav Bhandari, Rajendra Arlekar, Prakash Raul Babu Raul, Chandrashekar Desai, Sharif Deshmukh and Chakradhar Jha from the BJP; Madan Naik, Ashok Dhawale, Sukendhu Panigrahi and Sridip Bhattacharya from the CPI(M); Dinkar Tawde from the NCP; Arvind Sawant and Sajjid Supariwala from the Shiv Sena; Mayur Borkar from the RPI; Subrata Mukherjee from the AITC; Dr Manmohan Vaidya from the Rashtriya Swayamsewak Sangh; Sayyid Munavvar Ali Shihab Thangal of the Indian Union Muslim League and also his followers Rinisha V., Mariamma Shareef K. and Mohammad Rabeeh Srambikkal for arranging the interviews with the latter. My deepest gratitude to Datta Iswalkar of the Mill Workers Action Committee; Zubair Azmi of Urdu Markaaz; Ravi Shankar Srivastav of the Bihar Foundation; a former member of the Praja Socialist Party, Mohan Keluskar; veteran journalist Chandan Shirole and many more, who preferring to remain anonymous, helped out in reaching out to their contacts and were of tremendous support, help and guidance till the very end.

Once again, a big thank you for being there.

ACKNOWLEDGEMENTS

A wise man once told me, 'Politics is easy; it is the people who make it difficult.' At the outset, I would like to thank this wise man for encouraging me to look at the way Indian politics is viewed and practised from a different perspective. This book would not have been possible without him.

I would also like to thank the many people whom I would like to call friends and well-wishers who have stood by me all these years during my time both as a political worker and also while reporting on politics and crime as a journalist and who are a part of this book in some way or the other.

My deepest gratitude to my teacher and critic M. J. Akbar for showing me that there is freedom in words and in truth. I am deeply indebted to Madhav Nalapat for always encouraging me. I would also like to thank Robin Banerjee, my friend, philosopher and guide for motivating me.

My family—husband Sanjit, daughters Tonoya and Toya for their constant support and patience, and soulmate Ratnakar for motivating and pushing me to finish the book on time.

I am also thankful to Manisha Mathews of SAGE for her encouragement and my editor Namarita Kathait for her guidance, without whom this book would not have seen the light of day. I am fortunate to have them.

1
MEASURE OF A POLITICAL PARTY

1 Minions behind a Political Effigy

While the success of any political party in India is measured by its ability to win elections, and interestingly that may remain one of the crucial elements in gauging its success, what does work in the favour of any party is its ability to attract and sustain the dedication and loyalty of its foot soldiers. The role of an ordinary party worker goes beyond its job description—he/she lays the foundation for the growth of not only the party but also its leadership. A large human resource for any political party comprises its frontal organizations, namely the students' wing, the women's wing and the youth wing, and the people managing these vital frontal arms of any political party play a very important role. The choice of leaders who are put in charge of such frontal organizations ultimately decides the fortune of the political parties, more so in the case of national political parties.

The foot soldiers often taken on different roles within several layers of the organization and tend to perform different roles day in and day out for the smooth functioning of not only the party machinery but many a times that of the leaders who run it. From being a fundraiser to gathering crowds for rallies, the men who are instrumental in running the show continue to remain in the background, often invisible or made to feel unimportant. Party workers or minions confess how they began their so-called 'political careers' by doing an odd job here and there for the party. Despite doing their jobs effortlessly, they realized that they had no position within the hierarchy of the party.

Both, Mayur Borkar from Maharashtra and Manohar Bothra from Madhya Pradesh share their stories on the different roles they have had to adapt to over the years to keep themselves prominent within their respective parties.

FROM STITCHING BANNERS TO ALLIANCES

A former Congress worker, 42-year-old Mayur Surendra Borkar, who is now with the Republican Party of India (RPI) claims that his association with politics was accidental; it began when he started creating cloth banners and designing of campaigns for candidates who stood for college elections. 'College is the first step of politics for both party workers as well as leaders. I was a student of Bandodkar College of Science, Thane and although a science student and an avid reader, I was creatively inclined towards other fields as well.' He further adds that he never participated in college elections since he never liked giving speeches. 'I loved designing and strategy and planning stuff. Soon I found myself actively creating and designing banners and election campaigns. I did not learn this art through any course but on the job itself. I began creating, designing banners and slogans on them. For instance, if a candidate is contesting, then how his slogan should read, how his photo must look on the banner, the photos of people who could be there with him on the banners and so on.'

He adds that most politicians take their banners seriously and hence one needs to be very careful when creating them so as not to upset them. 'One needs to look at all angles—like that of caste or whose photo should come first—when designing banners for politicians. Sometimes there used to be mistakes like a picture of a prominent senior leader would be replaced by a nondescript person and then all hell would break loose. I did all this till my first year.'

Mayur narrates how he soon became friends with a group which included a few Congress supporters and Member of Legislative Assembly (MLA) Kranti Koli's son, Mangesh Koli. 'At that time, 15 years ago, although Anand Dighe of the Shiv Sena had a stronghold in Thane, the Congress performance was quite good and they too had created a strong base for themselves there. Hanging out with Koli and his group, I almost became a dropout. They appointed me to a position in the Youth Congress at that time. I remember Balkrishna Purnekar was the Youth Congress President then. I was given the task of designing and putting up banners and flags for the party. I used to make cloth banners, not the flex banners that are popular today. Cloth banners used to cost ₹3 to ₹4 per square feet, though now flex banners are cheaper.'

Putting up banners too is an art and exercise in itself, he continues. One should know how to put it up properly. 'The angle and direction of the banner too were crucial and depended on the stature of the leader; one had to keep in mind when he was coming from Mumbai to Thane and which road he was taking to travel. The senior leaders would always appreciate my banners. Balkrishna used to show them off to the leaders who in turn would applaud me for my work. I never spent on these banners from my pocket. The party used to pay for them. Making banners soon became a part of my source of income.'

Now decades later, Mayur is an important man in Mumbai's strategy media circles and is known to handle the political portfolios of several leaders including the portfolio of Ramdas Athawale, the National President of the Republican Party of India (Athawale) (RPI [A]). Mayur points out that college is where most youths begin their association with politics. He believes that working for any political party is a full-time job and becomes difficult for people with 9 to 5 jobs to survive here. At times, there is no source of income while contributing one's time for the party. Mayur says, 'For a person in a full-time job, whenever there is a protest or a *morcha*, then he has to take leave from the office. People working in shifts at their jobs find it difficult to juggle between office and party work together.' He adds that every party worker—when he joins politics—needs to select his role within the party appropriately. Each one should understand one's capabilities and act accordingly. 'Not everyone needs to carry flags, you need to identify your qualities and then plan your path accordingly. Not all are destined to become leaders. Not all are bestowed with the talent of giving good narration or speeches. Every leader needs to have the support of a lot of people to get there. Like my friend, Mangesh—he could accommodate everybody in his life. When he is around there are no fights. Even today, his supporters would come and stand for him in his time of need. But for me, it is not so. I am very particular about my work. . . .I realized that to survive in politics, I needed to make money out of my banner and hoardings business and that is what I did. Similarly, one can opt for handling public relations of leaders—for instance, social media is big these days and party workers can look in that direction for their line of work as well.'

POLITICS AND CONNECTIONS

Mayur points out that his work of creating banners brought him close to other parties as well. In the Shiv Sena, he became acquainted with Anand Dighe, a Shiv Sena leader from Thane who had a very strong base there; soon Mayur joined him along with the other boys from the Congress. Mayur says that he was in the Congress party for merely two to three years and had joined the party not because he followed its ideology but because he had friends who were in the party and they took him in their fold.

In the Shiv Sena, Mayur did not stay for long as Anand Dighe too had passed away by then. But, since he desperately needed money to run his house, he continued giving banners to other Shiv Sena leaders whom he met during his stint there. 'When I was in SSC, my father left us and it was left up to my mother to handle everything herself for me and my brother . I remember those days when I used to work the whole night and would go to railway stations and eat *vada pav* to satisfy my hunger. I would work the whole night and again feel hungry the next morning and have *vada pav* again at the same railway station, where I would have put-up banners the whole night. Even that one *vada pav* would be divided between four to five people. We never had money back then. I decided that if I had to stay in politics then I needed to create something for my survival and hence started my line of banners. At that time, flex banners were introduced in the market and it was a good opportunity to do something too.'

Mayur reminisces of the first order he got from Ramdas Athawale. It was his father who had referred him to Athawale as he used to reside at Siddharth College, where Athawale too used to stay at that time. After that, there were many other side orders from the Congress party too. His business, he states, continued the whole year through and was not just restricted to elections. There were programmes of the Seva Dal, another wing of the Congress party. By the time that got done, there were orders from the Nationalist Congress Party (NCP) for their *jayanti*s. At that time, Mayur could easily make a profit of ₹15–20 thousand, every month.

Mayur says that he has noticed over the years that people are initially enthusiastic about joining political parties, but gradually they are disappointed when they realize that they have to invest money and they give up, 'It happens a lot of times that most workers don't get paid, or some get paid less. Even I was disappointed like them at one point but fortunately, the few clients I had did not make me realize my loss or let me me suffer; they used to pay the money for the work done.'

PLAYING DIFFERENT ROLES

Political alliances are a part and parcel of Indian politics today and Mayur claims he was fortunate to be one of the main crucial links in the formation of one of the major political alliances in the state—the BhimShakti and Shivshakti aimed to bring the Hindu and the Dalit votes together. 'I got into the PR job by accident. It was around the BhimShakti–Shivshakti meeting. Post this meeting political movements began happening fast. When the alliance was announced, all media turned up there enquiring who would speak on these happenings. All Shiv Sainiks at that time shared my number with the media persons and I found myself juggling numbers and fixing appointments on who should speak to which channel and who will represent the party in the debates. And from that day onwards, I began my public relations for Athawale. Post the alliance, whenever there were protests or press conferences by the party, I used to advise Athawale on various issues of [the] media. I learnt PR on the job; I did not go to a PR class or learn a course like today's youngsters do.'

THE ART OF MANAGING LEADERS

Mayur states that one needs to have some political sense to manage a leader, 'I have seen two types of public relations (PR). One is being a PR and other is being a spokesperson. They are two different things. Today we have both spokespersons and PR rolled into one. This is not correct. Today, the PR has to be behind the scene rather than sit in front of the TV; if anything happens, he has to inform his leader about it. With social media around and a lot of things going viral, he has to be alert at all times of the many incidents that could happen. Often good news gets buried under rumours so one has to take care of that too. 'A spokesperson cannot be a PRO (public relations officer) and a PRO cannot be a spokesperson. The work of a PRO is to remain behind the curtains to get the work done. These days, whenever their leader speaks in front of the camera, the PROs stand behind him and are more interested in whether they are visible or not. I don't like that. If I roam in cars with leaders it is only to talk about press releases and nothing else. Once you become a PRO, you have to be only a PRO. I can appear in media every day because I have good connections but I can't contest the elections. Contesting elections is a different art altogether. Personally, I will never contest elections because I know that will never happen. I am not ambitious. My work is related to PR and hence I will do PR. I don't think I am fit to become an MP or an MLA, I cannot do that at all. But many others believe they can.'

He points out that in this age of social media, everyone believes that they can do PR, including leaders themselves, but people don't take such things seriously. Some political leaders think, he says, that it is unnecessary to appoint a PR and spend money. They believe they can also do it and type four lines on WhatsApp and circulate it. 'But I strongly feel that leaders should do the work of leaders only. By typing four lines and circulating it through WhatsApp isn't going to get your PR done. These days, leaders sit in their cars and tweet. But they should realize that even their tweets should make sense. They have to be composed in such a way that people understand the tweet and that the tweet becomes a hit. For social media, you need to create a good poster, have good photos, etc.'

So, does good PR help win elections one may ask?

To which Mayur responds saying that PR does play a major role in winning elections. The strategy, he says is planned in this manner, 'Like in the case of the Lok Sabha elections, we count which constituency consists of which community of workers. But if you see the PM Narendra Modi's campaign—his campaign wasn't specifically targeted towards any particular community—whether it was Muslims, Dalits or Brahmins, everyone joined in irrespective of the caste.... It wasn't strategy but good marketing,' he adds.

Mayur believes that the protests are part of the fundamental rights and many-a-times, necessary. 'Whether you are in the opposition or at the Centre, if you see something wrong then protests are necessary. Unfortunately, these days, protests are staged not for a cause but to get something in return. In the past, protests or *andolan*s were based more on emotions but today these protests are for the survival of a party. The Bhima Koregaon protests that took place in Mumbai was a spontaneous reaction. It wasn't an *andolan* but a reaction from a particular community.'

Strategizing, he claims, is an important part and merely shelling out news through WhatsApp cannot get one anywhere. 'You need to create strategies as per particular moments arrive. You need to think on your feet. Speeches are important and so does what a leader has to say. The party workers always need to be motivated too. You need to keep the party workers busy so that they remain committed, active and bound to the party. Only then can a party perform.'

Athawale, he says, does not allow his party workers to sit back and relax. He keeps a programme for them every day. 'There are other parties who don't have any programme. Merely staging anti-protests isn't a programme at all. The leaders need to be in touch not only with the public but also the lowest worker. In Maharashtra alone, you will find leaders opposing each other publicly in the mornings but will gather for a function in the evening and celebrate together. You can find this only in this state compared to the other states where forget attending functions, they don't even invite anyone of their own. This is what is called healthy competition.'

GETTING AHEAD

Although Mayur believes that women can do much better in politics, he points out that the situation for men isn't easy either. They find it tough and competitive. 'I have observed that in politics, the first thing is that no one allows anyone to go ahead politically. If the party sees that a person is very active, then they don't see that he should be appointed on some committee in which way he can do good work which will, in turn, benefit the party. They don't do that. They try to stop the person then and there only. Secondly, I have also seen that they put up competitors. For example, if I am good at my work, the party will prop another candidate against me. What happens is that we end up competing against each other. At times, the leaders themselves instigate this.' He claims that the leader is the only one who benefits from this rivalry. Today, creating such kind of competition and rivalry for this generation is harmful. If a political party needs to stand on its own and grow independently, one needs to take everyone together. For political parties to become successful, the age is gone where two competitors are pitted against each other; today everyone needs to work together if one wants to succeed.

Casteism is yet another factor that drives Indian political parties and unfortunately also the base of Indian politics. Mayur claims he has never experienced casteism at all in the RPI. 'The RPI is mainly a party for the poor. A majority of the party workers are from slums and every worker is known to richly contribute in his way.' He does add that in the Maharashtra political scenario alone, there are six to seven Dalit factions currently active in the state who promote themselves in their unique way. 'Most of them believe that they can face the media on their own and don't need PR. That is a misconception they all have. You need different skills to survive in a political party. It's not like you dress up in a white shirt and white pant, gather some boys, take out a *morcha* and shoot the entire thing on a video.'

The Way Party Workers Are Treated

Mayur believes that most party workers are fully utilized in politics. 'When the Bharatiya Janata Party (BJP) wasn't in power, there weren't too many party workers with them. Now that they are in power, the flow of party workers to the BJP has increased. And if such a huge lot of workers are in the party, obviously not everyone can be accommodated. Naturally, leaders use them to their fullest capacity. They are promised positions, tickets, promotions, etc., given the responsibility to conduct programmes like Shiv Jayanti or any other religious events whenever needed. But workers too should be smart to understand what they are doing.' He further observes that the problem party workers face is that when they join a particular party, they become way too committed. Some people are sly and cunning. They know the tact of making money. No party gives money to any party worker to spend on expenses. In some rare incident, if the worker meets with an accident, gets disabled or has some problem at home then he is given help. During elections, the party may help him with some funds, like banner expenses, etc., but the party will never spend on his entire election campaign. This is why when selecting candidates, the full background of the candidate—including his financial one—is screened by most parties.

There is also the question of maintaining good relations. 'If I am new to the BJP and I am given a particular area, then I would be required to build a good rapport with whoever is heading that area. If I am contesting the elections, then I need to build a good rapport with him, I will have to be in his good books,' says Mayur. Party workers, he feels should pick a stream they are comfortable with. 'I picked the line of public relations. Tomorrow if my boss tells me to contest, I will not, because I am a PRO. I will do the job of electing any person in a constituency from Panvel and Mira Road well.'

Mayur believes that the rich creamy layer of Dalits does not go to RPI but to the Congress party instead. 'They don't like to be called Dalits. Both IAS officers and senior bureaucrats who are Dalits have the money and are often seen joining the Congress party even though they know they can't get anything in that party. In RPI, the problem is that the party is not in power. Because it isn't in power, it cannot give the party workers anything. Because we are in a coalition but don't have the whole power—whatever we have, we are expected to share with others and hence accommodating our workers becomes a problem. But these Dalits at the top always want something in return. They always need to have something. They tend to believe they know the political trends and feel that if the Congress comes back in power in these forthcoming elections, they would benefit from it. For these so-called big people" all of this is a time-pass. They are not fully devoted to work for the party or society in large. You may have senior IAS officers with money, but their utilization is not there.'

THE ROLE OF WORKERS AND GROUPISM WITHIN POLITICAL PARTIES

For 63-year-old Manohar Bothra, a former member of the All India Congress Committee (AICC) and a delegate of the Madhya

Pradesh Congress Committee (MPCC), the survival and success of any party worker in Indian politics is dependent on which camp he belongs to. Bothra who has held several positions in various committees—from being a nominated director to the State Bank of India in three states to that of being on the advisory panel of various industrial bodies of the country, believes, that irrespective of whatever role you play in the party, your success is mostly dependent on your relationship with the leader and the coterie he commands and how useful you are to him and his political career. 'Post the death of the late Prime Minister Narsimha Rao in 1993, groupism increased in the Congress party. Things like "Don't give a ticket to so and so guy because he is that leader's minion or his man was common to hear", this "cutting to size" of the worker began from the post-Narsimha Rao government only and continues even till today.'

A former media professional, Bothra, who originally hails from Ujjain, began his political journey from the city after his graduation in Bachelor of Arts in 1971. 'There was no one in my family from politics. At that time, I came in contact with the Mayor of Ujjain, Satyanarayan Joshi who incidentally initiated my entry into politics. I had accompanied him for a rally to Delhi that same year where I befriended Prakash Chandra Sethi, former Chief Minister of Madhya Pradesh. He had contested from Ujjain. We hit it off immediately and soon I was accompanying him everywhere. I was merely 18 years old then. Soon, through him, I became a part of the Youth Congress, the youth wing of the party,' he recalls adding how he soon ended up conducting programmes for Sethi and also accompanying him everywhere.

'Prakash Chandra Sethi was an honest Congressman. He worked with dedication and was sincere and loyal to the party. When he lost the elections in 1989, he vacated his bungalow within 8 days and shifted to Ujjain. There are very few politicians like him in this country who would do that.' He narrates how he was deeply influenced by Sethi's honesty and has, over the years, tried to imbibe his qualities in his life as well. 'I had decided then to work honestly and dedicatedly in politics, whether you get something or not and maybe that is why till date I believe I haven't got anything concrete in my political career,' he laughs. He continues that how through Sethi, he came in touch with Motilal Vora, who at that time was an MLA from Madhya Pradesh. Vora too, he says, was a very dedicated person and deeply influenced his life, 'Even today (he is now the General Secretary of AICC), I am in touch with him.'

'It is very difficult for me to forget my loyalty towards Sethi*ji* (with whom I was associated with till his last day) and Vora*ji*,' claims Bothra, who soon formed his circle of political alliance-cum associations with other leaders like the late Madhavrao Scindia and Sushilkumar Shinde. Bothra used to work at *Samachar Bharti*, a newspaper in Delhi in the early eighties when he first got acquainted with Scindia. 'I had come to know that he was staying at Hotel Claridges in Suite No. 111 and one fine day I just walked up to him at his hotel to talk. Scindia*ji* was from Madhya Pradesh from Gwalior and was deeply attached to Ujjain as the latter was under his "rule". He had newly joined the Congress party and I was interested to meet him. He was quite strong and prominent in Madhya Pradesh politics and used to help a lot of people during elections. After our first meeting, I began accompanying him to Parliament where I got to meet a lot of leaders from other parties. I soon managed to make good connections with many of them.' He clarifies that unlike present times, leaders then used to be easily accessible to the common party worker.

This system of meeting leaders with appointments only, he informs, came into existence after the death of Prime Minister Indira Gandhi, 'Till before the Narsimha Rao government was formed, workers within the Congress had a lot of enthusiasm for their party. After the death of Rajiv Gandhi (whom I had met twice), and after Narsimha*ji* became Prime Minister, there was a lack of enthusiasm amongst party workers. The only saving grace at that time for me was Sushil Kumar Shinde who was appointed the Observer and General

Secretary of Madhya Pradesh. Shinde*ji* had a quality of making himself available to meet workers at all times, even in the middle of the night if need be; there are very few politicians like him at the national level who prefer meeting people very easily. For instance, it was also quite easy to meet Arjun Singh, another big Congress leader. He too was accessible and used to meet a lot of people.'

Bothra says that after 1993, with the appointment of Digvijay Singh as the Chief Minister of Madhya Pradesh, there became an increasing number of groups and camps within the Congress party, 'It all started in Madhya Pradesh during the election of the Chief Minister. Both Digvijay Singhji and Subhash Yadav were aiming for the Chief Minister's position. But on the orders of Delhi, Digvijay Singh was made the Chief Minister and from then onwards, not only did political interference from Delhi in the state's affairs begin but so did the formation of groups and camps with the party. There was a split in the workers; while some went along with Digvijay Singh and some opted to stay with Arjun Singh, others owed their allegiance to Vidya Charan Shukla. These camps are in existence even today. He points out that the common party worker suffered immensely due to such groupism and camps. Their confidence took a hit and many workers were soon relegated to the background.

Rajiv Gandhi, Bothra says, did a lot to promote the party worker but after the BJP came to power and Congress lost, the Congress workers started getting demotivated. When Congress did come back to power in 2005, groupism and camps within the party were at its peak. Madhya Pradesh was split into the camps of Digvijay Singh, the Shuklas and that of Arjun Singh. When the new state of Chhattisgarh was founded from Madhya Pradesh, a further three to four groups—that of Arjun Singh, Digvijay Singh, Scindia and Subash Yadav—came into existence within the party in that state.

Bothra adds that camps are founded to promote their own people and create hurdles in the paths of those who differ with them and also with the sole objective of being in power. Although there were efforts by Scindia to bring these groups on one platform and finish the rivalries between them, unfortunately, that did not happen. These camps are alive and kicking even today.

Groupism, he says, will cease to exist only when the leaders believe that it is the party which is one and above all. 'Until Delhi *wale log* do not take stringent steps, groupism can never end. The one who is working against the party should be removed immediately. These camps function as separate power centres. It is not only a question of which group has more money but which camp can get most of its men adjusted to key powerful positions within the party hierarchy. For example, during elections, instead of sending one list from every state, camps send their separate lists to the Centre.'

Bothra points out that in the eighties, leaders treated party workers with love and respect and that the Congress party, did not have any 'high-flying' politics which one witnesses today. Common workers who used to travel to Delhi to meet their leaders were usually taken care of by the MPs in their homes in the capital. He says that today the number of MPs who make arrangements for their party workers are very few. Bothra, who used to earn a meagre salary of ₹500 as a marketing professional of the *Free Press Journal* newspaper in Bhopal, used to stay in the home of MP Babunath Solanki whenever in Delhi. 'Like myself, many workers used to generally stay in the MP's house where their one-time meal and tea and accommodation would be taken care of. Earlier Parliamentarians used to do a lot for their workers. I remember the house of BJP MP Hukam Chand Kachwai, who was also from Madhya Pradesh, being flooded with Congressmen. He was an MP first from the Jan Sangh party and then later had been elected from the BJP. His residence, 19, Windsor Palace till he remained in office, never closed its doors on anyone. Workers cutting across party lines used to gather at his home. At that time, there were no camps—there was a feeling of *aapnapan* or togetherness in those days. The leaders used to listen to their problems and help them out. Today, a party worker finds it difficult to even make it to Delhi and survive on his own. He not only has to make his travel arrangements but also has to spend on his accommodation, local travel, meals, and also set up appointments with the leaders, etc. No *neta* helps a party worker anymore. The ones who do get help must surely be the ones having excellent access to the parliamentarians.'

While a majority of party workers find solace in being close to power and powerful people in politics, there are an equally large number of people who are desirous of having power by demanding tickets for themselves during elections. While some end up being successful in their attempts, the ones who do not, soon find themselves adapting to different roles within the party in the hope that their fortunes may reverse someday.

Bothra claims that he too had always nurtured a desire to contest elections but could never really connect with anyone for that matter because of the many camps prevailing within the party. 'I had demanded a ticket for myself in 1998 but soon realized that it is very difficult for party workers to get tickets in the first place. I was a victim of internal party politics. The ones who distribute tickets first see which camp you belong to. For any worker to get a ticket was a big thing.'

Bothra adds that money alone cannot get one ahead in the party— rather it is the equation with one's leaders. One cannot get a ticket unless one has close relationships with the people at the helm who are entrusted to hand out election tickets to candidates. Unless one is not close to any one leader or part of any camp, it is impossible to get a ticket to contest elections.

Due to this, he says, the value of an ordinary party worker in the party is on a decline. Every leader wants that his stooge should contest and win and in this rivalry between leaders, the genuine party worker suffers. They do not get any attention and importance that they once used to get. The situation is so grave these days that the appointments of even local and state positions such as district presidents, delegates, etc., too are decided by Delhi and not by state representatives.

'In such cases where will the common party worker go? This is not the approach of a worker! In many cases, the worker has no access or does not even know any big leaders. What will the party worker who is supposed to work for the party do then?' questions Bothra who confesses that his survival within the party was by his own efforts. 'I learnt to adapt to the people I met. There are many party workers or minions who hang out with ministers just to be close to powerful people. They hope this association will get them business or money. While some do benefit from this association, many others do not. Getting government contracts, business or a government agency to run is often the goal of many common workers who hang around with the *netas*,' he says. He also says that he is not in favour of leaders handing out charity but wants them to encourage and motivate the workers to get ahead.

He believes that the party worker was the happiest during the rule of the late Rajiv Gandhi. He mobilized party workers in a big way. He used to promote them at all levels. Opportunities were made available to the common Congress worker during the tenure of Rajiv Gandhi which incidentally was not available during any other time. At the Nehru Yuva Kendra for instance, many workers got a chance to work there. Rajiv*ji* he says, was a very honest man. He wanted that every Congress worker should reach each village across the country.

The Nehru Yuva Kendra did a lot of work in the deep interiors of many villages. At that time, young Olympian hockey player by the name of Aslam Sher Khan was made a minster and he too encouraged many people to go ahead in life. But unfortunately, Khan became a victim of party politics and internal groupism; today he is nowhere within the party hierarchy.

'Every state follows its kind of politics. A worker can do politics in any state because his intentions are honest, noble and his purpose and goals are clear,' he points out adding that the Congress generally conducts membership drives which are a gateway for common workers to get entry into powerful positions within the party. Workers admitting members in large numbers are often awarded a post in a committee like the Pradesh Congress Committee (PCC) or AICC. Interestingly, he says, there are also many workers who despite putting in the efforts, lose out on such opportunities. 'At the beginning of my career, I too had registered the highest number of members (who pay a fee of ₹25) and I failed to get any position. When I stopped making members, I was inducted into the AICC,' he laughs.

●●● ——————— ●●●

The first law in Robert Greene's book *48 Laws of Power* (2010) highlights the importance of appreciating one's master and never outshining them. The law aptly states, 'Never Outshine the Master: Always make those above you feel comfortable. In your desire to please and impress them, do not go too far in displaying your talents or you might accomplish the opposite—inspire fear and insecurity. Make your masters appear more brilliant than they are and you will attain heights of power.'

The stories of Borkar and Bothra are sheer examples of how these dedicated foot soldiers leave no stone unturned in seeing that their masters excel at what they are doing and achieve great heights. It should be noted that running a political party requires not only the dedication but also the support and skill of people from different backgrounds. Not all are destined to be the leader, but they are definitley destined to take their leadership ahead. Keeping this in mind, when parties invest in nurturing these 'silent workers', who while remaining behind the scenes endlessly and tirelessly work towards realizing the dreams of their leadership, such political parties are sure to flourish.

2 Political Loyalty

In an unabashed display of love and affection to their leader, Mayawati's repeated victory in the Uttar Pradesh elections in 2007, party workers and supporters of the Bahujan Samaj Party (BSP) raised funds to erect a plush three-storey building in suburban Mumbai in Maharashtra. The building, nestled in a Sindhi-dominated neighbourhood was inaugurated as the state headquarters of BSP in 2011 by Mayawati herself and had since then witnessed over 200 visitors a day until she was in power. The fully air-conditioned building decorated with Italian marble also served as a museum with Mayawati's bedroom, bathroom and face tissues drawing visitors in large numbers. The bathroom was a combination of gold and white Italian marble with the glass wash basin golden in colour. While huge bronze statues of Mayawati and BSP founder Kanshi Ram decorated the corridor on one floor, the former chief minister's meeting room was decorated in colours of blue, pink and adorned with huge glass chandeliers that kept changing colours. During the evenings every week, Buddhist preachers would sit outside the BSP Bhavan singing prayers for Mayawati followed by distribution of offerings of *kheer* prepared by them.

People who came in large numbers to see the bathroom and the bedroom used by Maywati*ji* were also offered a guided tour of the entire property by office bearers of the BSP. The latter believed that the people who gathered to see the building were her true supporters and it was their right to know the progress the BSP had made till date in the state. Many party workers believed that the visitors were also proud of the fact that a Dalit woman had achieved so much. Another party worker of the BSP informs that the bathroom where Mayawati*ji* took her bath was no less than a shrine and BSP supporters were found kneeling in front of the bathtub as if offering prayers. 'They regarded *Behenji* as their god,' he said.

Idolizing their political masters and elevating them to the status of gods is nothing new in Indian politics. Leaders, too, seem to enjoy the fact that they have a huge following and they make no bones when it comes to showing off. Even after the death of the leader, it is the common party worker who is entrusted with the task of keeping the memory of the leader alive. For instance, in the state of Tamil Nadu, loyalists of the late superstar and politician M. G. Ramachandran or MGR as he was called, show no signs of forgetting him. Even though the state is currently witnessing the attempt of two superstars to grab the political space—namely by Rajnikanth and Kamal Hassan, the aura created by MGR's All India Anna Dravida Munnetra Kazhagam (AIADMK) seems irreplaceable and continues even today.

LOYALTY TO A PERSON THAN AN IDEOLOGY

Trinamool Congress leader and Minister for Panchayati Raj, Rural Development as well as Water and Development, Subrata Mukherjee points out that the idea of loyalty differs from person to person. While some party workers remain loyal to the party, others may find their loyalty in the leadership and not necessarily in the ideology of the party. He cites his own example where his close association with the late Congress leader and minister from West Bengal, Priya Ranjan Dasmunsi proved to be a changing point both in his personal life and his career. The 69-year-old recalls how he came across the charismatic leader during his student days at Bangabasi College where they both studied.

'It all started with student politics. I wasn't from Kolkata but from Burdwan district and had joined Bongovasi College to study history honours as a Bachelor of Art student. I had no personal goal or ambition to become a politician. My father was a teacher and we hailed from a middle-class family. Normally, to be a politician is a luxury for any middle-class family, and since my family did not have any political connections, they did not have any idea of politics or any ambition for the same,' he says. Rather, he nurtured a desire to be a naval officer and was pursuing the role of a cadet captain of the naval wing of the NCC seriously too. 'I had enrolled myself in the cadet-camp training course and from there on, had gone for training for two to three months on the INS *Brigade* and later on the INS *Mysore*. After my training in Panjim, I appeared for the direct officer examination in the Navy but couldn't succeed. My second attempt too did not materialize. I decided that maybe the Navy was not for me and while all this was happening, I became friends with Priya Ranjan Dasmunsi who was in student politics at that time and also a leader of Calcutta University's Students Union. Dasmunsi was my senior while I was still in my third year. He was, at that time, promoted to the position of Chief of Youth Congress, a Congress-sponsored students' body.'

His friendship with Dasmunsi proved to be his entry point in Indian politics. Subrata recalls how it was a tough time to be in Kolkata in those days and more so ever in Bengal politics mainly because of the Naxalite movement which had emerged in the late sixties and early seventies Despite that, he was very much influenced by the politics of Dasmunsi and gradually began involving himself in his political programmes.

'Since, due to the Naxal movement, it wasn't safe for both to travel back and forth from our homes to the college every day we began residing at the Chhatra Parishad office where we came up with the idea to establish various wings of the Chhatra Parishad in all colleges across Kolkata,' he informs further adding that Kolkata in those days was largely dominated by the Communist ideology and there were hardly any Congressmen in the state. But he was oblivious to all of this and his association with the Congress was mainly due to his close friend and mentor Dasmunsi. 'I was influenced by Dasmunsi and that was the only reason I joined the Congress party. At the same time I did not go into the details of what the party stood for and how beneficial it would be for me politically, etc.' he admits. At that time, the Naxalite movement was one of the tensest ones in West Bengal at that time where students, judges, teachers used to be killed every day by the Naxals and it was very difficult to survive in this atmosphere. Around this time, he continues, elections were announced and it was during his second year of graduation, that the Congress party offered him a ticket to contest elections from their party.

'It was 1971 and I was still a university student when I was offered to contest from Ballygunj which is in South Kolkata. I was merely 24 or 25 years old at that time,' he says crediting Indira Gandhi for this decision. 'Indira*ji*'s thought was that the youth should come in politics and she chose many such young people and gave them tickets too. In Kolkata, both Priyamda and myself were fighting against the Naxalites and because of our courage, many students became our fans and I believe that is why both of us got elected, Priyamda became an MP and myself an MLA.'

But the victory was short-lived as in 1972 they had to face elections again where the Congress won with a majority. Subrata adds that it was a big achievement and he was soon included in the ministry. He was the youngest minister in the country at that time.

'I was less than 25 years old and in power. It was a learning period for me as I tried to learn how an assembly works and functions, what my duties are, what am I supposed to do, how do I learn the system, how to talk with the IAS officers . . . my idea was to learn from everyone and everything. Inside the cabinet, too, I used to remain quiet and observe how other senior ministers and people talked. Although I was young, I was a senior minister in the government and I was entrusted with one of the most important portfolios—the home department!' But the taste of power was short-lived when Subrata lost his seat in 1977; he blames 'Delhi politics' and groupism for this.

'I was always attached to the idea of a national party and not a regional one. At that time, the so-called groups and camps in the party were almost negligible. Siddharth Shankar Ray was the Chief Minister then and as a leader, he was in the know of everything that was happening in West Bengal. And at the national level, there was Indira Gandhi. She was accepted by the people and everyone in the party. I lost that election marginally because of the Emergency but was re-elected in the elections that took place after that.'

Although Subrata's journey began from the Student's Union as the years went by, he spearheaded other important positions even though the CPI(M) remained in power. From being the Chairman of the Public Accounts Committee to overseeing the trade union movement, Subrata did it all. 'The activities of the trade union movement in Bengal had terrific impact on the society in those days. I became the Indian National Trade Union Congress (INTUC) President at that time in Bengal. So, from the students' union to becoming an MLA to a trade union leader—all of this was only possible because I learnt from a lot of seniors in the party and also mainly because I was very close to Dasmunsi. I learnt many things from him. I was also very close to other leaders like Siddharth Ray (from whom I learnt a lot as well) and also Indira Gandhi and her son Rajiv.'

SHIFTING LOYALTIES

From 1971 till the time Mamata Banerjee broke away and founded her party, the All India Trinamool Congress, Subrata remained with the Congress party. 'I did not join her initially because Mamata had walked out of the party alone and it was very difficult to join her then. At that time, I was also the working President of the Congress,' he says. He moved out of the Congress party because Dasmunsi became sick and was hospitalized for almost eight years leading to a big vacuum in the political space.

He is not ignorant of the fact that Mamata had initially worked under him and that he is now reporting to her. 'When I was in the Congress party both Mamata and myself fought together against the CPI(M) party in West Bengal. Mamata left and founded the All India Trinamool Congress Party and started a terrific movement against the CPI(M). At that time, she was the leader against the CPI(M), not the Congress. The fact that she had left the Congress party to fight against the CPI(M) wasn't lost out on the public who accepted her as their leader. She was the face who was opposing the CPI(M) and the people accepted that. So that's why a few years later I joined her,' he informs. Mamta had worked for her victory when she was nominated a Member of Parliament (MP) on a Congress ticket. 'When the Congress had nominated her for MP, I was the General Secretary of the party and had worked for her. People used to know that she is my candidate. Both of us worked together as a team,' he continues pointing out that he did not mind the role reversal when he joined Mamata's party.

'One has to keep one's mind open. Although Mamata is my junior in politics I would still say that she is my leader because the people have anointed her as their leader. It is similar to that of Indira Gandhi, she was junior to Morarji Desai and yet people regarded her as their leader. Even though she came from a dynasty background she was accepted by the people. When Mamata attends a mass meeting to speak, the crowd swells to almost 10 lakhs but when I do the same, hardly 50,000 people turn up to listen to me. So, it is eventually the people who decide who will be or is the leader. When Indira Gandhi was getting her foothold in the Congress party, there was a lot of debate on this internally, but it was the public that regarded her as their leader. Morarji and the others at that time could not accept it and that is why they were finished,' he analyses. Thus, one has to accept the voice and choice of the people.

In West Bengal, particularly, he believes the people decide who their leader will be. 'The leader is decided by the people and not the party. The people's opinion is more important than those in the party,' he cites giving few examples like that of the late Communist Party leader Jyoti Basu whose acceptance amongst the people was more than that amongst his party. 'The reality is that while the party may decide on who will be Number Two and Number Three, the Number One position is decided by the people. This is a reality and you have to accept it. I have accepted the fact that Mamata has been anointed by the people as their leader and is more important than me. That is a hard reality. It is not that I was a contender, or she was working under me, etc., etc. Based on her work, Mamata has been accepted as their leader. When I got elected for Mamata's party for the first time, it was because of Mamata's vote not because of any Congress leader's vote.'

The party, he says, is important but also equally important is the leadership. The person leading the party too plays an important role because the leader is the face of the party.

And in West Bengal, as well as other parties, that is a problem. There may be strong parties but none like that of Mamata. 'The Bharatiya Janata Party (BJP) in Bengal too has no leader of its own; similarly, after Buddhadeb Bhattacharjee, the former Chief Minister of CPI (M) stepped down after the party's defeat, there has been no leader from the party. But, Mamata has been here because people have faith and confidence in her party.' Subrata regards himself as a team player and does not mind that he is now working under Mamata. 'At one time she was working under me and now I am doing the same,' he smiles confessing that he has no desire to leave his regional space to pursue any higher prospects in national politics.

Conflicts, he believes, are also a part and parcel of the 'loyalty package'. He points out that over the years in his political career with both parties, he has come across incidents when at times, the people in leadership positions have been wrong and he has pointed this out to them. 'Sometimes your assessment about many things is right and there have been times when I have brought this to the notice of the people concerned. When it is a party issue, you can sort it out internally but when that becomes a public issue it tends to create controversy. Sometimes you have to adjust to what the leader believes in and swallow your pride and continue doing what you are supposed to do,' he adds. Walking away from the party or opportunities, he says, is not a very good thing to do. One has to be honest and consistent in what you do—both in family and social life. Although he misses Dasmunsi, Subrata does not mind leaving the Congress since he adds that he was in the party only due to his close association with the late leader. But he does find a lot of differences between the two parties.

'The Trinamool is more regimented than the Congress. The Trinamool party's followers have no culture of showing off. Dasmunsi was a natural leader and my meeting with him was just one amongst the natural course of things that took place in my life,' he adds. Like Dasmunsi, he too had been following in the latter's footsteps by guiding those who come to him for advice.

'I can identify leadership qualities in those who come to me. That is a god-gifted power that I have. There are a lot of people who come to me and express their desire to be with me. I keep a keen eye on them, the way they behave, their approach towards others, their attitude, etc., because eventually, he will be regarded as my man and if a person does things negatively, that will affect me and my name as well. Though I may notice his loyalty, honesty and approach towards others, in the end, the person has to prove himself in his work,' he sums up.

●●● ———————— ●●●

Subrata's views on loyalty and leadership might not necessarily be shared by others. Sixty-two-year-old Chakradhar Jha, a long-time member of the BJP believes that there are various shades of loyalty that one gets to witness in one's political career. A resident of Bihar, Jha shifted to Mumbai in his youth and shuttles between the two states. Seated in his quaint office, which stands within a sea of high-rises on one side and slums on the other, Jha says he prefers calling himself a Maithil more than a Bihari. A BJP loyalist to the core, Jha goes down memory lane and explains why he has attached himself with the BJP for so many decades.

'I come from a small village called Pariharpur near Madhubani district in Mithila, Bihar. More than calling myself a Bihari, there is more prestige in calling myself a Maithil. Bihar was destroyed by politicians. From the beginning alone, Bihar is an imaginary name which has no base. Bihar was made after combining a lot of cultures. Mithila is more cultured compared to Bihar. It was the birthplace of goddess Janaki—wife of Lord Ram, poet Vidyapathi, Yog guru Yogacharya Patanjali, Rishi Kapil and Sanskrit scholar, Vachaspat. We even have our separate calendar called Saur named after the sun which is similar to the calendar of North East India.'

He claims he was forced to run away from Bihar due to an incident that took place in which he was not even involved in the first place. 'I was in college at that time. My name unfortunately figured on the list of students involved in the student protests which were part of Jayprakash Narayan's movement in Bihar. When my father, a farmer, came to know of this, he told me to leave everything and go away from there. If I had stayed there, I would have been killed. So, in 1975, I came straight to Mumbai from Bihar. And then Emergency was declared.' He recalls that when he first came to Mumbai, there was no BJP, but a party called Jan Sangh. It was the time when the Janata Party too had not been formed. He found shelter with some relatives from the village who were staying in the suburb of Mulund in Mumbai and to survive, began doing odd jobs for people in the community—like helping in making ration cards or if anyone had a problem with the municipality, etc.. . . . I often used to wonder about my situation. While back home, my role was more of an activist protesting this and that, in

Mumbai, I was transformed overnight into a social worker and more of a helper. I think it had a lot to do with my father who too was inclined towards social work and did a lot of it in our village. I was young—about 20 years old. Then the elections happened.'

Since Jha had left his studies and fled to Mumbai from Bihar, he couldn't study further. His first job during the elections was helping out in putting posters on the public walls across Mumbai. All newcomers were required to do this. He claims he generally used to go out in groups around midnight to do this and his task used to be to wash the walls and create the base for writing political slogans or creating posters on those walls. 'The Jan Sangh party had no money and all of us used to pitch in to help to create the publicity campaigns. I used to wash the walls, while someone else from our group used to mix the lime and create the base on the wall for writing slogans, while another member would later write on the walls.'

Later on, the Jan Sangh and all other parties, except the Congress (I) party, merged to form the Janata Party. When the BJP was founded in the early eighties, they needed party workers. At that time, he was introduced to a party worker called Mishra*ji* from Uttar Pradesh who told him to work along with him. At that time, Jha claims he did not know much about the party or its functioning. When the BJP was established, there was a lawyer and advocate Mohan B. D. Chandani, who had contested the corporation polls from one area of Mulund colony. There were hardly 20 to 30 houses in our area Amar Nagar who would know BJP, but Mohan had got votes of a few houses from that area. And from then onwards, they started the process of enrolling the locals as members of BJP.

'Around 1982–83, I got a job as a senior supervisor of a construction company. I used to work eight hours a day and earn around ₹400–450 per month at that time. I used to contribute my time for party work only during elections and also voluntarily. The reason I involved myself in political work was that I always liked to be in touch with people. I believe that every person has an instinct that defines him and what he wants. It is a part of what nature has instilled in us and my nature was to be around people, to mix with people. See, I have been a stage artist at one time. It was more of a hobby. I used to dabble in acting in Hindi theatre as well as write poetry, songs and even dramas. I used to show off these skills at the local community gatherings many a time.'

Jha adds that then again, another set of elections arrived and he began working in the campaigning of BJP leaders like Jaywantiben Mehta, Pramod Mahajan and Vamanrao Parab. He says he is deeply indebted to the latter who gave him an opportunity to be more active and entrusted him with the responsibility of the entire area. At that time, there was a concept of *basti pramukh* and the organization appointed him as one; there, he did a lot of work for them by bringing in several people into the BJP. At that time, people were reluctant to announce that they were supporters of some other party than the Congress. When Jha put up the BJP flag on his house, some goons attacked his house and tore up the flag. When he went to the police station to complain against them, he was the one who was jailed instead. Not a single BJP leader at that time came to help him out, he says.

The reason he stuck on with the BJP despite all these problems was because of their idea of Hindutva and his belief in that ideology. He claims that BJP, at that time, did not take any workshops or classes to prompt people like him to follow this ideology of Hindutva. Today, he continues, the BJP does not need party workers anymore. This is because elections are now contested and won by the name of only one person—Narendra Modi. No elections are won in the name of the candidate alone. The strategy of contesting elections has changed. Party workers were needed before Narendra Modi came on the scene. Modi is now the headline—the person who will win is Modi and the person who will lose is Modi. He believes that the party now instead wants rich and loaded party workers. 'The BJP was the most democratic party at one time, now it isn't. But whom do people like me, who are at the bottom level of the party hierarchy, can complain to?' he questions.

He admits that he disagrees that only those who raise money for the party are given importance. The importance of a worker, he claims, is based on several factors. 'Other political parties have asked me to join them. I am very active on social media and very aggressive too. I don't spare anyone. In the recent past, I was invited by the opposition parties to comment against the BJP on social media and get paid for it as well. Since several other parties are also on social media, a prominent party at the Centre offered me money to write against my party. The money was huge but I declined. It was against my principles. I believe that in politics, one has to go beyond one's own rules and principles. If you need to stay in politics, then you are required to do everything and anything that is demanded of you to stay in power—*saam, dham, dhand, bhed* or simply put 'by hook or by crook'. You need to be able to do good things as well as the not-so-good things equally, without which you stand no chance of surviving in politics ever. To protect one's territory and position, leaders resort to desperate measures to hold on to their seats. It may be easy to win, but it takes great efforts to stay put and a leader will have to do everything that it takes to survive and hold on. An honest worker has no place in politics and should not even enter politics. The structure in politics today is that there is no place for honest men here. There was once upon a time—before Independence and even post Independence for a decade. Now the speed at which the state of politics has declined is alarming. It has become dirty and unbearable,' he trails off.

Loyalty as a criterion for recognition and promotion, according to Nadeem Nusrath, former National Secretary, Indian Youth Congress and ex-Chairman, Mumbai University Students Union, is not just confined to politics. It exists in every sphere of life right from hiring a domestic servant to the corporate sector. And the recent example of the same is the Tatas where Ratan Tata's own appointed Chairman was dismissed for not toeing the line which amounts to loyalty.

Nusrath believes that although the loyalty factor is largely seen in the political sector primarily because that is the only criteria to hire and judge a person—academic merit holds whatsoever no charm in politics. However, he continues, it must be noted that of late, loyalty as a criterion has completely collapsed in mass-based parties where ideological moorings do not hold weight. In ideology-based political parties—especially the right-wing parties—loyalty to ideology is far more pronounced than to the individual political leadership. The problem with mass-based political parties like the Congress, the Samajwadi Party (SP) and other regional parties is that one hardly gets to see content and ideology-driven political leadership or rather one hardly witnesses content or ideology-driven meritorious men and women attracted to these political parties.

'Therefore, the only criterion which is available to the leadership of these political parties is the loyalty criterion. And this is the biggest bane of these political parties because as we see today these political parties have loyalists but none of them can counter the ideologically driven right-wing political parties. The communication wing of the Congress party is the biggest example where loyalists were given top positions, but in the face of not being given political power, they quit the party to join the right-wing diametrically opposite-driven party. Meanwhile, the others who are managing the communications department were unable to weave a narrative because the only criterion for their selection and in turn the criterion for the selection of their team was the loyalty factor! When the chief of the communication department is barely able to secure his security deposit while coming third in a state election, then it is important to realize that loyalty by itself has no place in politics just as it has no place in the corporate sector,' he explains. Nusrath believes that loyalty and merit, especially academic merit with a proven track record of understanding the concepts at play and how to apply them in various sociopolitical models must be necessary criteria besides loyalty in politics which the Congress, in particular, must put into practice. 'Having said this, it is also important to note that dissent should not be construed as disloyalty. It is important for political leadership to appreciate issue-based dissent and not to judge a dissenter as disloyal,' he observes. It is, therefore, important that political parties, especially in their formative years or when they are in power, must pay extra attention to creating a loyalist cadre which is intelligent and content-driven.

'This is so because the political parties neglect their organization and human resource while in power and then a weak human resource is entrenched in the party hierarchy purely based on muscle and money power. This is very difficult to change when the party loses power and struggles to create a counter-narrative that is acceptable to the people.'

●●● ——————————— ●●●

When political leaders tend to go beyond their own rules to accommodate the people they work with into their lives, friendships are forged. These friendships then, often go beyond the call of duty. In this day and age, when loyalty comes at a price, it is rare to find and even rarer to know that there are people like Subroto Mukerjee and Chakradhar Jha, who both being at opposite ends of the pole in ideology and culture are yet similar in their own ways. Both practise their forms of loyalty and make no qualms about it. While Subroto accepts the loss of his mentor by transferring and dedicating his loyalty to Mamata's party—a bold move for someone of his stature to do so, Chakradhar on the other hand, who has come to accept the reality of his position in the party continues to be loyal to it only due to the belief in his principles. Because he realizes that when one's principles are stronger than oneself, betrayal of any kind is impossible.

3 Ideological Cloning

The growth of any political party is dependent on its party workers or foot soldiers. The latter are responsible for not only propagating the programmes of the party to the common man and the voters but they are also indirectly the face of their party for the general public. What they do and what they preach is closely watched and followed. Which is why it is very crucial for political parties to not only identify workers who show an interest in their ideology but also those who will continue to remain dedicated and loyal, despite the ups and downs that the organization may face in the long run.

A majority of workers across different parties, when interviewed for this book, claimed that their association with a party of their choice happened for different reasons. While some said that they were invited by friends and acquaintances already connected to the party to join them, others pointed out that it was on the insistence of their family members already holding positions within the party structure that prompted them to enrol in the party as members. Some confessed that it was the personality of the party leadership that they were drawn to in the first place and not just the ideology of the party alone.

THE IDEOLOGICAL MYSTERY

While it is quite difficult to understand the reasons why different party workers follow different party ideologies, the primary common factor that connects them is that they do not just want a pat on their back by the leader, they also want political recognition, and a piece of the cake—the cake being 'power'.

An example of this is the 'mutiny' unleashed by workers of the Indian National Congress (INC).

In the general elections of 2004, against all odds, Congress party workers backed Sonia Gandhi, (now Interim President of the INC) and despite overall projections of the Vajpayee government returning to power, ensured a Congress victory. Similarly, in Maharashtra, the Congress, even after two successive terms was ensured a third term in office only because of the zealousness of its party workers. In the 2014 general elections though and some months later again in the state assembly elections, workers deserted the party because they felt betrayed when rank outsiders from right-wing political parties were accommodated in national politics and the party in Maharashtra did not release the much-awaited list of appointing special executive magistrates where no educational qualification was required.

'The Congress parties had no dearth of workers. Because it is one of the oldest parties, it naturally attracts everyone unlike the NCP—an offshoot of the Congress founded by former Congressman Sharad Pawar—which although has a large number of leaders, faces a shortage of dedicated party workers,' observes a party functionary on conditions of anonymity. Congress spokesperson Nizamuddin Rayeen says that there are no orientation programmes for newcomers who join the party. Party insiders say that student and youth wings of the organization are sometimes made to attend training programmes to promote the party ideology. Older party workers, at times, are taken care of by individual leaders in their capacity. In the Congress party, the common party worker is expected to learn the ropes of local and national politics on their own. Loyalty to the party alone is not enough; workers end up to picking and choosing the profitable side. They decide which leaders they have to

be close to and work accordingly. Caste too plays a role here as often Dalit party workers side with Dalit leaders and Muslim workers with Muslim leaders and so on.

●●● ——————————— ●●●

A similar trend is visible in parties that practise minority politics. Senior political journalist, Chandan Shirole says that while Dalit parties do not have membership drives, a majority of party workers believe that since they are born as Dalits, they invariably end up supporting any party that promotes the Dalit ideology. 'In Maharashtra, when a Dalit is born, he is made to believe that he is automatically a lifetime supporter of the RPI,' he says. They are not offered training of any sort but just asked to accompany their leaders instead when needed. Most Dalit workers love showing off their connections with their leaders and hence, they are more inclined to show their loyalty to the leadership than to the party the leader represents, he says.

PARTY WORKERS AND THEIR MAINTENANCE

Unlike the Congress, the BJP and the CPI (M) invests a considerable amount of time and effort in nurturing their party workers mainly because they are cadre-based. Capacity-training programmes are conducted across all districts including local levels to empower them. To keep their cadre updated on the developments, these programmes are well documented and widely publicized through many newsletters and periodicals that both parties frequently publish and circulate. The BJP is largely supported by the Rashtriya Swayamsewak Sangh (RSS), its parent body. Although the RSS office bearers deny the relation between the two, a large number of BJP party workers over the years have been promoted and elevated to various political positions with the support of the RSS.

Dr Manmohan Vaidya, *sahsarkaryavah* of the RSS informs that the RSS is not a political party and neither does it promote the BJP.

'Any political party can approach us. It is just that since the BJP has been seeking our advice and support on a lot of things over the years, people tend to believe that RSS is supporting only the BJP, which is not the case,' he says. He hands me a book, *About RSS—Rashtriya Swayamsewak Sangh*, published by the organization, which mentions that the RSS was established in 1925 and conducts social work across all states and districts of the country through its 40,000 *shakhas*.

An excerpt from the book states,

> The RSS has its own vision and concept about our national development. And our Swayamsevaks naturally have an inclination for such political parties who share this Sangh view and will be supportive of them. As the BJP shares this vision of the RSS, naturally it receives the cooperation and the backing of Swayamsewaks. The Swayamsewaks would extend their support to whichever organization or party that shares the Sangh vision. Hence we see BJP getting good support wherever the Sangh has a strong presence. However, the Sangh is not working for any political party, but it works for the whole nation.

Apart from its headquarters in Nagpur, Maharashtra, the RSS has set up its training centre in Bhayandar as well. Founded 25 years ago, Keshav Shrushti, the 200 acres lush green campus is located 40 kilometres away from Mumbai city and provides training to RSS and BJP cadres from across the country and abroad.

Taking a cue from this, the CPI (M), one of the oldest parties in the country which too boasts of a large cadre, also set up a centre in Kolkata to train its comrades. The five-year-old Promod Dasgupta Education Centre located in Kolkata, West Bengal is a permanent residential school for Communist cadre and offers guidance and training programmes to its comrades located across 22 districts in the state. Sridip Bhattacharya, General Secretary and member of the Central Committee of the CPI(M) informs that the party conducts frequent training programmes for members of its district committee. The residential school charges a fee as minimal as ₹150 per member for these programmes where party officer bearers along with the elected representatives are called to address the workers.

Sixty-three-year-old Sridip is a full-time activist of the party. His association with the CPI(M) started during his student days. An engineering graduate from the Bengal Engineering College (now known as Indian Institute of Engineering and Sciences), his journey with the party began when he first became a member of the Students' Federation of India (SFI), the youth wing of the party and was later elevated as its Secretary, Howrah District in 1973. 'Post completion of my engineering degree in 1978, I joined the party as a full-timer. The party used to pay me a small remuneration for my services too,' he says adding that his family wasn't too happy about his decision but they finally gave in. He says that party workers are asked to pay membership fees. 'As per our principal stand, we don't take money from capitalist people or companies . . . for the party and to carry out its day-to-day activities, we need money. There are two ways of money collection—either, we directly go to the people to ask for funds or we seek funds through every party member. Any member of CPI(M), if he or she is earning, whatever his or her wages, will have to pay a levy to the party. And there is a percentage on that levy. The percentage varies on the income of the party worker— for people who have wages less than ₹1000, their percentage is low, but for the people whose wages are more than ₹10,000, their percentage is higher. For the people who earn more, their levy also becomes higher.' Sridip explains that the rules for seeking funds from the party workers are as per the party constitution which mentions that all members of the party have to pay a certain fee.

He adds that the CPI(M) does not run on someone's will but the constitution of the party. If any member fails to pay the levy for three consecutive months, his or her membership ceases to exist. 'This discipline has been installed within the party. This has happened at times so we keep reminding our party comrades whenever they fault for three months to be careful,' he states.

•••————————•••

Political parties that invest in creating a membership force not only aid the party in propagating its policies and programmes but also in governance. A qualitative membership force also at times tends to reduce the party's dependence on alliance partners who have a committed membership base that is bound either by economic factors or an ideology. For example, party workers of the NCP are bound to the party's vast cooperative society's network as well as to the Yashwantrao Balwantrao Chavan Pratisthan popularly called Y B Chavan Centre which manages the tribal education network.

While workers of the All India Trinamool Congress are driven by strong an anti-Left ideology, the BSP has a committed ideology-driven membership of Scheduled Caste members and a very strong Labour union. 'When the BJP was in power at the Centre, they assiduously made a lot of appointments of their members or sympathizers at various levels of the judiciary. When the V.P. Singh-government was in power, the BJP ensured that Arun Jaitley, to increase his stature and standing, was given a top assignment as a law officer of our country. That investment helped the BJP when Arun Jaitley resigned and campaigned for the BJP,' says Nadeem Nusrath, former National Secretary, Indian Youth Congress and ex-Chairman, Mumbai University Students' Union. Nusrath, in 2009, has written a letter to the party demanding that the Congress too needed to create a databank of such members/ sympathizers who would work at the basic level of the judiciary, 'I had written that the Congress too needed to ensure that just as the BJP takes keen interest through the RSS in having their members get into the judiciary and influence public opinion, and makes these law officers then resign and join the party after gaining a certain stature to help influence public opinion, we could similarly explore this strategy.' He had requested the party to ensure that when they recruit members for the National Students' Union of India or the Youth Congress or when they are appointed as office bearers, the party should identify at least some of them according to their interest and potentiality as to which profession they could be accommodated in at a future date.

'I had suggested that as it is the party spends a lot of money on human resources—their travelling, accommodation and official visits, helping them understand the socio-political developments throughout the state or country but with no clear objective as to how the party is going to utilize and reap its investment. The whole exercise then reduces itself as an ad hoc measure,' says Nusrath. According to him, every party needs to explore—especially at the stage when they appoint office bearers through its student unions—how that young member is retained by the party for his lifetime.

'Not all of them are interested in becoming legislators. It is important to remember that in the BJP this activity is performed by the Akhil Bharatiya Vidyarthi Parishad (ABVP) President who is a college professor. The Communists, on the other hand, do not have any age criteria in their frontal organizations,' he concludes adding that members accommodated at important levels of the party's democratic structure become its vehicles to propagate its policies and programmes.

'Besides agitations and political programmes, parties need to have party sympathizers at the right places to influence public opinion as is so vital in any political set-up.'

A PARTY WORKER'S TAKE ON IDEOLOGY

In the eighties, the Indian Union Muslim League (IUML) was 'ruling' most Muslim pockets in South Mumbai. But, at the beginning of the nineties, the party's dominance was crippled due to prominent Muslim leaders defecting to the Indian National Congress (INC) and the newly formed Sharad Pawar-led (NCP). The party, today, is negligible in the city (it is a force in Kerala though) except for a select few who continue to follow the party ideology believing it can be revived. Like the IUML, every political party at some point of its existence has witnessed exits that often tend to cripple the very infrastructure of its organization.

Sajid Kassam Supariwala, a resident of Dongri (who later shifted to Agripada, Mumbai Central in South Mumbai) had joined the IUML sometime in 2014. He shares his story on how he desperately tried to revive the party from scratch but in vain. Unable to resurrect the IUML, he went on to join the Shiv Sena in the following months.

The 46-year-old belongs to the Supariwala family, which he informs has close links with the Memon community. 'Our surname is a famous one. My grandfather was a landlord of many properties in Mumbai. Our family were exporters of betel nuts. Though the Supariwala family originally hails from Jodia near Rajkot, Saurashtra, we were proper *Mumbaikars* because my grandfather and his whole family had shifted to Mumbai decades ago. We rarely go there now, and are *pucca Mumbaikars*,' he clarifies. He says that while 90 per cent of his relatives are in Mumbai, the rest have shifted to other countries like South Africa and London to pursue their livelihood.

'The Memon community has been renowned for their commitment towards the upliftment of society and almost everyone within the community has contributed to the construction of masjids, mosques and dargahs that you see across Mumbai today. Their history shows that they have always been helpful and donated a lot of money to social causes. The community has been a peaceful and helpful one and have immensely contributed to India's freedom struggle as well. When Subash Chandra Bose needed some funds for his fight against the British, there was the Gujarati Muslim Memon businessman, Abdul Habeeb Yusuf Marfani, who donated one crore rupees to him which was a huge amount at that time. The spirit of the Memon community is no different today,' he says.

Born and brought up in Dongri, Sajid says he was witness to all kinds of colourful lives that people led. He attended St Joseph's High School in Umerkhedi. Dongri, he says, has been a melting pot for people of diverse backgrounds and cultures and incidentally, it has also been the place for few famous and infamous personalities—businessmen, lawyers, doctors, gangsters, you name it. Ironically, it was also the same place where an invisible divide between Muslims and Hindus was always present. Elections, he continues, were a big deal in Dongri and Sajid has been witness to many over the years. As a child, he claims he used to pitch in for the local candidates by running within the many small galis of Dongri with their placards and banners.

Sajid continues that in Mumbai, the IUML was actively prominent in the mid-eighties right until the beginning of 1990 after which the party was completely wiped out, 'It was famous in Dongri. The reasons are not known but looking at their 'extinction' then led me to believe that if you are in politics, you constantly need to keep doing something or the other to let people know that you are around. At one point in time, there were many corporators from the party in the BMC. They had prominent leaders such as Sohail Lokhandwala, Yusuf Abrahani, Bashir Patel who later shifted loyalties to other parties like the Congress and the NCP.'

Since Sajid was already doing social work by helping NGOs, he had created goodwill for himself amongst his local community. One fine day, four years ago, Sajid claims he was approached by some people from the Kerala state unit of the IUML. The party being strong in Kerala, they had noticed him and his work within the community and wanted to involve him in their mission of bringing back the lost glory of their party in the city. Also, around that time the corporation elections too were round the corner and the IUML believed the timing was just right to re-enter the political scene in the city by contesting these elections. Since they were offering Sajid a position in their party, he agreed on the condition that he would work independently and without any interference from other people. He was soon officially appointed the Vice-President of IUML in Mumbai.

'This experience made me realize the difference between a party which is stable compared to a party which has been wiped out. The difference is that no amount of money is sufficient to revive a political party which is dead and gone. It would require too many funds to re-establish it. So whatever money, I was spending, it was always less,' he says. As he was quite well-known known in the area, when people came to know that he had officially joined the IUML, they approached him with offers of work. Many of them were excited—to create advertisements, banners, etc., announcing the re-entry of the party in their *mohalla*. But unfortunately, it appeared that what Sajid had planned for the party did not take off smoothly. 'It was very difficult to get things done in IUML due to lack of coordination and hence I quit the party,' he says.

JOINING THE SHIV SENA

Sajid confesses that he decided he would rather go to any other party but the Muslim League and during that time he had created his gathering of 4,000 workers who were ready to follow him wherever he went, 'Since other political parties too were noticing my work, lots of heads of political parties approached me to join them but since I was interested in the Shiv Sena (and was approached by Haji Arafat Shaikh who earlier headed the transport wing of the party), I joined them and that is how I became a Sainik.' He is now is the Vice President of Maharashtra Shiv Vahatook Sena.

Sajid recalls that post the 1993 Mumbai riots there were no Shiv Sena *shakhas* (small party offices) in the Muslim areas of Mumbai, especially in South Mumbai. He believes due to appointees like him, the numbers of *shakha*s have risen and more are currently being set up.

'As far as the 1993 riots is concerned—which impacted Muslims and Hindus in a big way—I believe that it is all in the past and time to move on. We are a multicultural country and we need to remain that way,' he says of his decision adding that although he was not in Shiv Sena earlier, he has always liked the idea of how they ran their party through the *shakha*s and now that he is a part of it, he is enjoying it very much. 'The Shiv Sena has *shakha*s all over the city even in its smaller by-lanes which we call galiis. I started meeting people from these small areas and galiis and built up my network by also visiting heads of wards and district—namely zilla *pramukh*s, *shakha pramukh*s, *vibhag pramukh*s, etc. A monthly cost of running one *shakha* can be anywhere between ₹10,000–15,000. While the *shakha*s were getting ready, our first investment started with creating awareness. We spent some amount on marketing, creating banners, placards, placing advertisements in the newspapers, etc.' He further points out that he has set up his office *sampark karyalaya* in South Mumbai's Null Bazaar area and has been approached by many people to solve their problems.

Sajid confesses that he was getting a ticket to contest the corporation polls but had to shelve the idea since he thought he was new in the Shiv Sena at that point of time and wanted to learn the ropes, 'I wanted to work some more time at my post rather than going in to become a corporator. My colleagues in the party also advised me to do the same, that to wait and do my work first and think of contesting elections later. But the thing is that it does not matter how many years you put into a party—that is not an issue. I have completed four years in politics now. But because I also come from a business community and being educated (I am a student at Wilson College), I am very fast in understanding and grasping issues. I have been witnessing many elections since my college days. I believe in the one year that I have put into the party, I have already invested an effort of 10 years. In one year alone, I have given 120 per cent of myself to the party, even during the corporation polls.' His entry into the party has helped the Sena win four seats—two Muslim seats and two Marathi seats right under the nose of the SP from a completely Muslim-dominated population which is a difficult task altogether.

MONEY AND ELECTIONS

Sajid believes that money is an important part of elections because, with money, one can get a lot of work done in such areas where you may be contesting from. Funding, he continues, is very important in elections, 'Whether you are contesting for the corporation, the assembly or the Lok Sabha polls, you need to have good funds in place to contest elections.' It all depends on the area that is the constituency that the candidate is contesting from. In some areas, a mere 25 lakhs will be sufficient while in others, even one crore is not enough. 'In my opinion, it is not at all feasible to adhere to the election commission's cap on spending—which states that only "this-and-this many lakh" should be spent on campaigning. One has to pump in money or funds—mainly from people who will help you out. Elections today are a costly affair.' He adds that the technique at how this money is spent too is different.

'All this money which goes into the sponsoring of elections doesn't happen at one shot. Say, if one has to arrange a meeting and book a hall for a rally, I would need to look at several things—like book chairs, book a stage, gather people for the rally. The latter would also need to be given food, drinks and water—all these things are collectively met with an infusion of funds. Without funds, how would one organize all of this? Plus, you would also need loudspeakers, and hence hire people to arrange for loudspeakers, a compere to make speeches before the start of the programme and many more such people. It is a huge and gigantic exercise that requires adequate manpower,' he says explaining that programmes hosted to promote the candidate during elections or otherwise are done mostly through sponsors. Rarely are cheques used as most of the transactions are in cash depending on how the funds are coming. It is very difficult to maintain accounts of who is keeping what—like confirmation of the venue, bringing in crowds for the rallies, their food, water, transport, etc. So, funds are mainly arranged through various states of implementation of the programmes during the campaign. A common party worker, he says, if he is a deserving candidate and in need of money—people will come forward and go out of their way to fund him in the elections. A candidate need not be from an affluent family; Sajid says that he has seen many candidates who despite not having enough funds have won elections.

He believes that the important thing is not all about winning elections alone. Positions within political parties too are an important thing to have to serve people, 'For example, if I hold a prominent position within a party, the poor, when they are in trouble do not approach any senior policemen or government officials, instead, they come to me for help. Similarly, if I want to get work done in my community or anywhere else, I approach government officials and they have to listen to me, they tend to respect the position I hold. People spend money in politics so that people can know them. If I am known to a lot of people, I can get work done. It's as simple as that.'

CRIMINALIZATION IN POLITICS

Sajid says that he would not like to use the word criminalization, as it is highly misappropriated, 'What happens is once when you are in politics, you need to be powerful and to have that power, you need to have people who are not necessarily goons but those who can defend you when the time comes. In politics, there is a lot of jealousy present. The more successful you become, the more people tend to get jealous of your success. You tend to attract rivalry too. When you are trying to do good work, you cannot please everybody and at the same time you also end up making enemies with anti-social elements. For example, if so-and-so is troubling someone and I come in to help that person out, obviously the person who is doing wrong will be against me. He would not like me helping the person whom he is troubling and ends up becoming my enemy. This is when we require people, such as security guards who can provide protection that is not easily provided by the state government or the police because it takes a lot of time for that. The police will provide security only if some incident happens or if they are sure that some incident is bound to happen. So, to save myself I would need to be surrounded by people who can defend me. They need not necessarily be goons but well-maintained and strong people, who can not only defend themselves but me as well.' The word 'criminalization' is, thus, given by people who do not understand what politics is all about.

When a leader or an organization is clear on what their party stands for and what they need to achieve, it becomes easier to attract party workers. While traditional national parties continue to operate under the brand that they have created, newer and smaller region-centric political parties often find it difficult to attract talent that is required to take the party forward. In the end, the objective of most political parties should be made clear to the party worker who needs to be trained accordingly.

The objective of most political parties is to win elections and seek power and to achieve that, political parties also need to invest in empowering the traditional party worker to do some out-of-the-box thinking for the same. Often, able party contributors are fickle, easily hurt and tend to get bored easily. When ignored or taken for granted, they are quick to shift not only their loyalties but also their ideas to rival parties. Hence, party leaderships should adequately take care that their workers do not feel that they have been taken for granted. Managing the ego of a party worker is a Herculean task and to achieve electoral power, political parties may often need to bend their knees to accommodate the same.

2
POLITICAL CAREER ROADMAP

4 The Life of a Political Worker

The survival of every political party is based on two major ingredients—its ideology or its stated stand on a particular issue and its party activists or rather its foot soldiers. The foot soldier is the first point of contact between the leader and the voter. The foot soldier or the political worker is not just a field activist but many things rolled into one—he is the one who influences the narrative in favour of or against his leader, he is someone who shapes the image of his party at the grassroots level, and he is also someone who can make or break the political structure of the party.

In a society obsessed with rejoicing the success of leaders and achievers, seldom are the achievements of such foot soldiers or party workers applauded. Their work is ignored, hidden behind the large political landscape, only to be picked upon for occasions that seem to benefit their political masters. Political parties survive or get decimated electorally when the apparent link between the party and its foot soldier becomes disenchanted or dysfunctional. Today, in modern India, the ideology of a political party remains a distant second.

Today, the life of an average political worker bears no similarities with those who laid down their lives for an independent and democratic India. Political workers cutting across all party lines have one thing in common—they do not want a pat on their back by their leader; they want political recognition, and a piece of the cake, the cake being power.

There are several factors responsible for the success of a political worker—the prominent one being the latter's connections and equations with his mentor and the ability and insight of exploring opportunities for growth. The second most important factor is the political worker's agility to survive in a highly competitive and toxic environment full of uncertainties and nasty surprises. This is the place where the most complex of human behaviours come to the fore. The capacity to manoeuvre one's way through a maze of insecure, unpredictable and opposing individuals of varied natures, each complete with an agenda of their own, is nothing less than an admirable skill which takes years to master.

For understanding, one can define party workers as per the following:

The Rural Party Worker

This political worker finds his common ground with leaders from his village or the surrounding area and concentrates on issues related to the rural belt—farming, price of crop or issues related to the village or farming community, farming land acquisitions, etc. They feel more inclined to be close to the party that seems to identify itself with their cause and issues faced by those residing in the rural belt of India. Often, rural political workers do not have much choice in choosing the party they often end up supporting the parties their local leaders are close to.

The Urban Party Worker

This worker is spoilt for choice. For the urban political worker, being part of a political party is more about networking and using the connections to make monetary gains. The demographic of an urban party worker may generally comprise people from diverse sectors like real estate, education, non-profits, entrepreneurs and those hailing from creative fields like art, cinema and theatre.

The Loyal Party Worker

There are two categories in this category—one who remains loyal to the leader and another who remains loyal to the party. Workers, loyal to leaders, do not give a damn to which party their leader belongs to and will continue to support him no matter how many times he may change the party, whereas, on the other hand, workers loyal to the party continue to be around the party under any circumstance.

The Full-Time Party Worker

This worker is entirely dedicated to the ideology and the cause of the party. Full-time political workers believe they are the whole and soul of their party and that they are required to give all of themselves to it. Many male political workers for instance, often vow to remain single than get married, all just to serve their favourite party.

The Part-Time Party Worker

He is the one who sits at local party offices or public-relations offices commonly called *jan sampark karyalaya*s in the evenings after attending to his full-time job. He is also the one who collects funds for his leaders from the locals for events and programmes hosted by his leader. This party worker finds solace in the fact that while he is not doing much for the party, he is making sure of flaunting his connections to the world that he is a busy man and makes time for the party whenever he can. Power brokers too can be slotted in this category. While some are loyal to one party, a majority of them shift their allegiance between several depending on the moolah they make.

The 'Staying on the Sidelines' Party Worker

This party worker neither has a membership of any party nor is loyal to any one leader or party. Instead, he remains at the side, watching and staying close to leaders and parties that come to power. His dedication is short-lived and fleeting.

The Election Party Worker

This category is known to become active only during elections. An election party worker is someone who uses elections to his full benefit. This is when party workers make the most money possible—through election campaigns, election rallies. Leaders contesting elections are known to spend astronomical amounts during campaigning and an election party worker is a godsend to them.

The Trails and Tribulations of Being a Party Worker

Political worker of the Congress party, Sushil Vasant Dalvi, a former District President of the Mumbai Youth Congress (the youth wing of the Indian National Congress ([INC]) reminisces how he was robbed of his chance of being anointed as President of the Mumbai Youth Congress the last minute when an opposite camp replaced his candidacy with one of their own. A worker with the party since 1993, and now 48 years old, Sushil still appears bitter about the experience and believes that the party failed him miserably.

'I had given everything to the Congress but realized that I had not been treated well. I was a fresh 22-year-old law graduate and the idea of joining politics first took shape after my many visits to the local Shiv Sena *shakha* (office) at BDD chawls in Worli where I used to reside,' he reminisces. The Sena, he claims, had a good stronghold in the area since many residents living here used to work in the nearby mills and the party had its trade unions attached to the mills,

'There was one *shakha* next to my house and I often used to wander in there requesting them to include me in the activities and programmes that they used to conduct. I had also expressed interest in joining their party but no one seemed to bother or gave me any favourable response. Around that time, I had also begun practising law professionally. A friend I was working with had a brother who was attached to the Congress party. When he came to know that I was keen to join the Shiv Sena, he asked me to join them instead and that was how I joined the Youth Congress.' The Youth Congress acted as an entry point for all young people to get into India's grand old party, the Indian National Congress. Sushil points out that many prominent Congress leaders—like Priya Ranjan Dasmunsi (the first president of the Youth Congress), Ghulam Nabi Azad, Anand Sharma, the late Gurudas Kamat—had begun their political careers from the Youth Congress itself.

Having been appointed Block General Secretary and his friend as Block President, they held programmes like distribution of notebooks (which was quite common amongst party workers and so was holding drawing competitions for school students), tree plantation drives, etc. Life, he says, began to change only when he met his mentor Rajiv Chavan, another practising lawyer and a Congressman. 'Rajiv, who was associated with the party, is responsible for pushing me ahead. When the position of District President for the Youth Congress became vacant, he lobbied for my appointment. At that time, in Mumbai, the president of the Mumbai Regional Congress Committee was Charanjit Singh Sapra. Rajiv had managed to convince Manish Tewari who was then the National President of the Youth Congress to have me appointed as District President. It was because of his networking skills that I was appointed as District President; otherwise, I would have been nowhere,' he says. At that time he realized that to rise within the hierarchy of the Congress, it was important to have people like Rajiv backing you. One could not be a lone wolf all the way.

Lobbying for positions is one way of getting into the party fold, he says. Important positions within the party are sought through intense lobbying through senior leaders and all those whom you can make happy. For example, if one is interested in becoming a District President then that decision rests not democratically within the party but in the hands of the National President. The workings are simple. First, your biodata goes out to him. He is made to understand that the person is already working for the party. The President is then informed that the candidate has been with the party for a decade or so and that consequences of the changes (both good and bad) if the candidate is appointed in that post. Even the national leader does not appoint someone directly but he takes the consent of local leadership. He asks local leaders whether the 'change' will create any dissent or not, and only then does he appoint the candidate.

Interestingly, there are no friends in politics. Sushil points out that in the year 2000 when he lobbied for his friend to be elevated to the position of the District President, he hoped he would be made Block President himself but was in for a rude shock. 'Just like any leader who plans to go ahead with his career, I too wanted to get ahead with mine and asked my friend to appoint me as Block President in his place since he had vacated his post. Instead, my friend began avoiding me and giving me lame excuses like "lawyers have no time to work for party affairs", etc. This was my first experience about the longevity of relationships in a party.'

He recalls how he had spent most of his time and money investing in the party—meeting both common and prominent people including leaders, travelling across the city on his scooter. At times, he claims, he was even required to host parties to boost networking. 'I couldn't afford to give parties at five-star hotels but would occasionally spend on investing in a biryani dinner which suited my pocket. This had helped me create a bond with them. These days such things don't happen. Leaders today entertain you only during elections. They offer you tea only when elections are round the corner otherwise you are as good as being invisible to them. The party used to have capacity-building programmes earlier but since the last decade or so, I haven't seen any such programme happening in the party,' he recalls. He had been rewarded by Chavan when he was appointed secretary in the MPCC.

Sushil believes that the Congress party needs readymade leaders. They prefer political workers from affluent backgrounds and investigate the aspirant's educational background, financial and social status, his / her family status, pedigree, etc. 'Your political road ahead will only be easier if you fulfil all of these criteria. If one expects that on joining the party, you can go ahead easily, then that is mere fantasy, it is impossible! You need to be financially stable in personal life to get ahead in politics. It is very difficult to go ahead within the party based only on ideology and hard work alone.'

No political party grooms leaders and certainly not the Congress. 'If you are not in a position to fill your stomach then obviously you will end up stealing in politics. Like said earlier, you need to be able to feed yourself, and be financially stable to get into politics. Having family members who are already in politics is a huge advantage but if there are none, then there is an immense struggle to go ahead. I have observed that even if there are good and capable candidates, without proper financial status or family backgrounds there is no way for them to get ahead within the hierarchy of the party.'

'Although I am a lawyer, there were times when people would ask uncomfortable questions about my source of income and myself. Law is a novel profession and I must confess that when I began making myself available to solve the problems of the people in the party office I would get questions from people like—'What does he do the entire day in the area?' or 'How does he run his house?' etc. It is embarrassing mainly because neither the people nor the leadership that you work for help you in any way. You are spending your own time and money.

He continues saying that a lot of energies are wasted in internal party fights. More than building a party of dedicated workers at the ground level, party workers spent a lot of time fighting internally. Most of these fights are supported by leaders themselves, who belong to different camps. 'The Congress party was very strong at that point and none of them went to the root cause of these internal fights and the reasons why they happen. Eventually, they weaken the political structure of a party.'

Sushil continues that it takes hard work to create and build a party or rather to sustain its existing image. 'Today, no one wants to join any political party voluntarily. It takes great efforts on our part to convince people to come and join us. There are very few people today who want to join the Congress too and the ones who do, come with many questions, most of them common in nature. They ask questions like whether the party would help them with money or whether they would get a post or what would their status be within the party? Would they be famous? I have seen that such kind of people do not stay in the party for long, neither do they survive for long.'

As for supporting the common worker, Sushil points out that the Congress party does not believe in either taking care or supporting the common party worker. This tradition does not exist at all. The old *thekedaar*s (caretakers) of the party live in this fantasy that the *praja* (public) belongs to them and them alone and that they are not obligated to anyone at all. They have no idea that the *praja* today has gone far away from them. They live in their bubble and refuse to accept this reality. 'This is not 1947 anymore. The Congress needs to realize this and wake up from their dream that they are not *malik*s (owners) of India anymore.'

THE GROWTH OF THE AVERAGE POLITICAL WORKER

While some workers, who despite rallying hard to be within their party's power structure end up sidelined or in oblivion, some are smart enough to chart their course and come out victorious. Unlike Sushil Dalvi, the rise of Congressman Kripashankar Singh was a phenomenal one, until he ended up becoming a victim of internal party politics and his flourishing political career almost came to a halt.

One of the most recognized names in the Indian National Congress party and more particularly in Indian politics, Kripashankar Singh's journey from a remote village in Uttar Pradesh to the power centre of Maharashtra politics is fascinating. A prominent figure to be reckoned with until tried and discharged from the multi-crore disproportionate assets case, Kripashankar discloses what his life was like as an ordinary party worker and the trials and tribulations he faced in his 35-year-long political journey.

'I have always regarded myself as a party worker more than a leader,' he begins recalling his journey from his birthplace, Jaunpur in Uttar Pradesh to Mumbai. 'I was born near Jaunpur in a village called Sahodarpur. Since childhood, I have been greatly influenced by my father, who was a village leader, a Pradhan as well as a freedom fighter. Our zilla was the only area where elections never happened and the locals would always elect my father each time on their own. We had a different atmosphere at home. My father, although a farmer, did a lot of social work and I believe I am only carrying my father's legacy forward.'

Second amongst three brothers, Kripashankar says he would not have come to Mumbai had he not been expelled from giving exams for three years. He recalls how a girl appearing for her Class 10 exams seated next to him in school had asked him a question from the paper; to help her, he had innocently written down the answer on a blotting paper which he was carrying at that time and handed it to her.

'Suddenly, the flying squad came in at that very moment and caught me. I got expelled from my school and disqualified for appearing for exams for the next three years! I tried hard to reduce my punishment from three years to one year but that did not happen at all. After this incident, I spoke to my elder brother, who was working as a sub-inspector in Excise in Bombay requesting him to give me a job in the city. I told him that being expelled from school and exams for three years will keep me off the education system and hence unemployed.

I wanted to work and in hope of finding in a job I landed in Bombay (as it was then known) on December 3, 1971.'

Kripashankar cites how hard it was to get a job then but he finally landed one in a French pharmaceutical firm called Russel Pharmaceuticals with a daily wage payment of ₹8 per day with weekends off. He managed to save ₹60 every month and after six months of working as an operator, he was finally elevated to a temporary position. The company did not make him a permanent employee though and this used to bother him a lot hence he shifted to another Switzerland based company in Mumbai called Roche Products Limited. Here, after fulfilling the required criteria of six months probation he was finally made a permanent employee of the company. He joined Roche in 1975 and worked for the company till 1989.

Kripashankar says that although he was doing a full-time job, he was always inclined to do something for the society and hence began to get more involved in his area in Jawahar Nagar in Khar where he used to live. He volunteered to clean up the surrounding premises in the evenings post work.

'I was staying in a very small house at that time, with four walls of aluminium and clay tiles for a roof, but I was much inclined towards cleanliness. I followed this belief that if Gandhiji could clean his own house then why couldn't I? Hence every weekend, and on holidays, I used to gather around 15 people and all of us used to clean the premises surrounding our neighbourhood that included the roads and by-lanes as well,' he says.

The Youth Congress had opened up its office where Kripashankar was residing and soon he found himself joining them. He began working with Harish Roge who was the Zilla President of the Youth Congress and all while continuing with his job in the pharmaceutical company.

He recalls his life-changing moment in 1977 when Indira Gandhi who had lost elections at that time had come to Mumbai. 'She was attending a programme in Kherwadi and I thought it would be a good opportunity to see her in person. I decided to bunk office that day and try to get to see her up close. Indira*ji* came to Khernagar in Kherwadi for an eye camp. Since she wasn't a Prime Minister then, she was not accompanied by any security guards. Seeing her from afar I started approaching her. I wanted to greet her with a "namaste" and touch her feet but saw that since I couldn't do so, I shouted out a loud "namaste" from a distance. She replied to my greetings with a "namaste" herself. Her response got me enthused and I felt this urge to talk to her more. I was aware that she used to contest her seat from Rai Bareilly in Uttar Pradesh and often used to rent the house of a person named Rai Dhunni Singh there. The latter's wife was incidentally related to my family in the state. I shouted out to her saying that "Dhunni Singh's wife is from our village and related to me." Indiraji stopped in her tracks, turned around and looked in my direction and asked me what I was doing in Mumbai. I told her that I am working in a full-time job. She asked me which district I was from and I said Jaunpur. She further questioned me whether I had a holiday that day to which I replied with a no, saying I had bunked office just to meet her and have her darshan. "How will you make a living if you have only my darshan?" she asked Kripashankar to which he replied that sometimes it is good to seek the darshan of gods and goddesses as it gives one the strength to go on. I told her, "Meeting you is a boost for me, it will give me shakti. I will do overtime at work to cover my lost hours." She said okay and advised me that if I wanted to work in politics, I needed to get out of the house more and do whatever good things I wanted to do. "Apart from your job, do not end up doing something that you are not proud of," she said. Her words inspired me so much that I began to work harder each day. When she became a Prime Minister two years later and had come to inaugurate the new assembly building in Mumbai, I again went to meet her reminding her of my Rai Bareilly connections. That time A. R. Antulay was the Chief Minister of Maharashtra.'

He continues that all that time he was only an active worker of the Youth Congress working for the party devoid of any post but was finally made the General Secretary of Kherwadi taluka in 1978 when elections were announced. He recalls how at that time it was difficult to get Congress candidates to even contest elections.

Kripashankar informs that while working as a party worker at that time, he had to spend his own money. The party did not ask for any money but all workers had to pitch in for the programmes of the party in the form of getting batches, flags, etc. He recalls that his meeting with Indira*ji* had triggered something in him and her words had struck a chord within. So, he immersed himself completely in social and party work.

'A regular schedule of mine would be to work on my job as an operator in the mornings while in the evenings, I would go to the party office sitting and sit there for half an hour or so. On weekends and holidays, I would spend long hours in the party office. On some weekends I used to do overtime at my office. I was the only North Indian in the firm while the majority were Keralite Catholics and Maharashtrians. My salary was good and since I did not have too many expenses, I led a very simple life. Slowly people started inviting me to make speeches. Although I did not pass my high school, I used to participate in debates in schools. The oratory was something that I had learnt from my father and I put that to good use at the party. My father was a Congressman and a freedom fighter and my family too supported me a lot when I was doing social work. My brother, a government official, had a limited salary but he never stopped me from pursuing what I enjoyed. He was always supportive of whatever I did.'

For nearly 22 years until Kripashankar became a minister, he stayed in the same small chawl in Mumbai where he had started his life from. In 1984, when actor Sunil Dutt was announced as a Congress candidate of the Lok Sabha, the responsibility of the entire election campaign was given to him. From that time onwards, he confesses he became close to Sunil Dutt and his role in the party became stronger. When assembly elections followed a few days later he pitched himself as a candidate for an MLA ticket. But unfortunately, he did not get it and Janardhan Chandurkar was given a ticket instead. Though disappointed, he worked hard along with others to get himself elected as MLA in 1985.

Post the assembly elections, the corporation elections followed and once again, Kripashankar asked for a ticket to contest the polls but was denied. 'I did not get upset. I always thought that if I kept working hard, I will get a ticket someday. The party will be forced to give me one if not today then definitely tomorrow! I thought that maybe the one who has got a ticket has made a good impression on the leaders and that I too should work hard enough to make a good impression. . . . Following that, I asked numerous times for a ticket to contest elections from the party but did not get it. Janardhan Chandurkar at that time was the President of the Slum Cell of North West district and he appointed me as President of the zilla of the North West. And I began working in that position. Around that time, I got introduced to Pratibha Patil, she was the Food and Civil Supply Minister of Maharashtra. She was a regular attendee at the Maharana Seva Pratap Mandal and because I became close to her, I would get problems of the locals of my area sorted through her,' he says.

'Just like a mother who teaches her child to walk, she taught me the art of "walking in politics". She liked me and always encouraged me. Whenever there was her programme in Mumbai she used to call me and I used to go. At that time, I used to give convincing speeches in her programmes. My relations with her deepened so much that I used to tell with authority to anyone who approached me with any problem that "Chalo, let's go to Pratibha Patilji and sort this out".'

During his tenure as Zilla President, people used to approach him with a variety of problems to solve—from rations cards to admissions, all of which he says he tried to do without ever leaving his job. He mastered the art of time management and took a permanent second shift at work from 3.30 pm to 11.30 pm after requesting the management. After doing political work in the mornings Kripashankar used to go to work in the second shift and come home post-midnight every night, have food and sleep for a few hours and then would be up at 8 a.m., have a bath, cook his food (because he did not have family staying with him) and begin his social work at 11 a.m.

Post noon, he would again take the train from the suburbs to Bombay Central, get down and walk all the way to Roche factory in Tardeo. He claims that because this was his daily routine, political work soon became a part of his life similar to brushing one's teeth every morning. Having juggled this life for nine years, it was in 1986 when Pratibha Patil was appointed Deputy Chairman in the Rajya Sabha and she also took over the mantle of the President of the MPCC. This was the beginning of new opportunities for Kripashankar. In 1988, he was given the charge of being the Organizing Secretary of MPCC.

When Vasantdada Patil was the Chief Minister and Murli Deora was the President of the party in Mumbai, Kripashankar's name was considered for a corporation ticket but overnight, the name of a small-time worker Sudarshan Mishra was finalized instead. Upset and angry at this treatment he claims he went to sign his form as an independent candidate from the same area. 'This also because I was instigated by people around me who said that if I wasn't getting a ticket I should contest independently. In 1985, I finally filled a form as an independent candidate to contest the corporation polls.'

At that time, Ramesh Dubey a Congress leader who also was a leader in the corporation called him and told him to rethink his decision to contest as an independent. Dubey told him that in case he won it was good but if he lost then no one would take him seriously in the party ever again. 'You will be removed from the party and then you will not be able to do anything ever. If you believe you can win, then you must surely contest,' Dubey told him.

Kripashankar says, 'I told him to give me a few hours to think and promised to revert. I recalled this conversation to all those who had asked me to contest as an independent candidate and realized that the same people who had coaxed me to fill the form, backed out when I told them about Dubey's suggestion. They refused to back me saying said that they could not go against the party and that I was on my own. I thought hard and realized that I was after all a common man. What if I lose? I had no money of my own to survive if that happened. Thinking about all the repercussions my loss would have, I withdrew my nomination. News spread fast that I had withdrawn my form. Again, I kept quiet and worked hard just like any other worker to make Mishra win and he won.'

He confesses that he did feel bad about the whole experience but who could he complain to about such treatment given to him by the party? Kripashankar says that no one could talk on his behalf. These decisions were made at the higher levels and that he had no access to anyone there at that time. The only people who knew him were those from his area and he could to put his grievances across only to them.

'There was an old block president called Shankar Gaonkar. He was senior to me but he too did not get a ticket ever. Similarly, there was a C. G. Gopalan, even he did not get a ticket in his life to contest elections. All of those who were senior to me have never got tickets ever and I wasn't the only one. I thought I needed to get ahead of all this and there was a lot of struggle in doing so. In the end, denial itself becomes your sole strength.'

Kripashankar recalls his days as a party worker. He claims that there weren't grooming sessions for party workers then unlike today. He too wasn't very ambitious and had no ambition to become a

Minister or an MLA but he always believed in one thing—if he was working for something, he should get a certificate for that. He should be accepted and applauded for it.

He admits that his main reason to contest elections was that if he got elected by the public, this would be the proof that they had accepted him and keeping this in mind alone, he worked hard.

'My family, especially my wife never complained about this. My wife, Malati never cribbed about me not taking her for the movies or elsewhere. I never even gave enough time to my kids. The contribution of my wife, who is my strength and my children have been immense in my life,' he says.

Although in rural areas caste plays a prominent role, he believes caste in Mumbai is viewed differently. In Mumbai, he says one is viewed as either a Maharashtrian or a non-Maharashtrian. This is experienced by everyone. Kripashankar says that he doesn't think that caste plays a role in politics. 'I could not have won three assembly elections if it had. I fought four elections but won three. From 1999 to 2014, I contested four elections. If caste was a factor then I wouldn't have won these elections in the first place. People from every class and background need to have proper representation. I have heard people say that Kripashankar Singh is a North Indian and that he helps the North Indian factor in politics. I cannot ignore that because I am a North Indian. If the party had a lot of North Indians, my efforts have always been that they should be properly represented and not ignored. But I always felt that I should do something that people should also regard me as their own. I think language is one medium in which we can go closer to each other. This is why I started reading the Marathi language through Marathi newspapers. I made a lot of mistakes but I have no regrets in speaking in Marathi. I also used to try to speak in Kannada as I had neighbours who were from Karnataka and similarly Bengali too because I knew a lot of people from Bengal. One must learn Marathi because it is after all the official language of Maharashtrians in Maharashtra! We shouldn't fight to make them realize that we are different but give them so much love and acceptance they will regard you as one of their own. The region which gave me so food, shelter and dignity how can I disrespect that? I always tell in my speeches that while Hindi is my Mother, Marathi is my Mausi (mother's sister).'

Kripashankar believes that the difference between politics then and now is that there has been a decline in our principles and values. The principles today are more aimed at winning elections at any cost—to take power at any cost! And when that happens, when you try to come in power at any cost, try to run a government at any cost; you tend to lose sight of what people want. Earlier the elected governments used to remain in power for many years compared to the governments today who are always on tenterhooks thinking in which direction the political climate would change. 'I have been a three-time MLA and it was during my fourth time as a candidate I saw how a wave of religion was unleashed and misused to gain votes. Different parties had put up different candidates to divide the votes. The Hindu votes were polarized, so were the minority votes too and in this way, I lost my seat,' he says.

He does believe that his political journey has been a fruitful and an interesting one.

'I have had the good fortune to be in the state assembly for 15 years. From 1994 to 2014 I was a minister and for over three and a half years I was the President of the Mumbai Regional Congress Committee. During my tenure with the Congress party, I was the general secretary for the organization from 1988 to 2000 and have worked with over nine party presidents during that time. I have had the honour as a party worker to work with Pratibha Patil, Narendra Kamble, Sushil Kumar Shinde, Shivajirao Patil Nilengekar, Shivajirao Deshmukh, Ranjit Deshmukh, Prataprao Bhonsale and Govindrao Adik. For four years between 1992 and 1996, I was the only General Secretary along with three

Vice-Presidents and one Treasurer in the Maharashtra Pradesh Congress Committee (MPCC) which had Shivajirao Deshmukh as its President. A committee couldn't be formed then due to internal differences between the members but during those four years, I travelled all over Maharashtra doing party work. I used to eat and sleep at Tilak Bhavan in Mumbai, the party's headquarters, every alternate day,' he adds.

Kripashankar points out that he does not believe in groupism and that the latter not only wreck the structure of the party but also cause loss to the organization. Party workers tend to lean more towards one single entity rather than the party itself. Interestingly, the party worker also suffers immensely because of this. If he becomes close to any particular group, he becomes an easy target of the opposite group and a victim of their politics. Party workers who resort to spreading rumours due to loyalty to their camps, over the years become disillusioned and they too meet with the same fate—they too end up becoming victims at the end.

'Although I have never accepted groupism at all, I was a victim of it myself when I did not get a ticket to contest elections for many years. I was never a part of any group but was often identified as being part of one—whether it was with Pratibha Patil when she was our President or with Vilasrao Deshmukh when he was the Chief Minister and I was in his ministry. I was a minister in Sushil Kumar Shinde's government as well. I followed the principle of following a group which has only one commander and foot soldiers like me—in my case following the Chief Minister. I believe not everyone can be commanders and that is how I have managed to work with nine party presidents. If I was a part of any group, I don't think I would have had this 35-year-long political journey. I don't think a common worker like me could have got this opportunity time and again,' he adds.

He continues that he was a party worker and will always remain one and will undertake whatever responsibility is given to him. 'When I got the responsibility of being an MLA I took it up, also when as a minister or president I worked equally hard for the party. Today I am neither an MLA nor hold any position in the party. I go and meet people like before, just like an ordinary worker does.

Sanjay, Kripashankar's son recalls the time when his father ended up becoming a victim of party politics and was dragged to court. 'Our family was the first family in this country to face the trial in the court-of-law. My mother and sister who are typical housewives are always in the kitchen and taking care of the family. They had nothing to do with politics and were dragged into this. I am not even a member of any political party and I was pulled into this God-knows-for-what. The only one spared was my daughter because she was one-year-old!'

Sanjay says that the behaviour of people too changed around them because of this. 'When the media were saying what they were saying, people believed them. The media took on the role of being the complainant, the lawyer, the witness and judge all at once! I thought to myself if the media thinks all of this, then surely I am the criminal! But fortunately, some good and honest reporters did their jobs well,' he says. He thanks god for getting them the justice that they deserved. Despite such upheavals, Kripashankar says that this hasn't left him disappointed.

A glance at the political roadmap of an average political worker tells a lot many things not only about himself but also the trials and tribulations they are subjected to time and again to prove their worth to the party and their political masters. The fact that we are constantly living in an unequal society isn't lost out to them when deprived of their share of respect and success in the party hierarchy.

The main reason for the decline of the Congress party across the country can be witnessed in the stories shared by Sushil Dalvi and Kripashankar Singh. Both built up the party machinery in their own ways. While Dalvi, who although being a local, depended more on his political bosses for his promotions and when denied remained mum about it, Singh on the other hand despite being a migrant worker in Mumbai, through sheer hard work and ambition, juggling both his personal and political life, managed to achieve the impossible. He was very clear that he wanted credit for his work and went out of his way to get it. Unfortunately, like in the case of Dalvi, it was internal party politics that brought Singh's (he was also an able fundraiser of the Congress party) political career to a stop.

The Congress party has many such stories of their foot soldiers who disillusioned with the party's functioning distanced themselves away from them. This brings us to the conclusion that foot soldiers play not only an important role in laying the foundation of any political party but also sustaining its success in the long run.

5. Political Godfathers and Dynasty Politics

Godfather—a term that not only arouses instant deep interest but also implies several connotations to it as well. Various versions of the English dictionary have given diverse definitions for the word 'godfather'—one defines it as a man who sponsors a person at baptism, while the second states 'Godfather means one having a relation to someone or something analogous to that of a male sponsor to his godchild.' Other dictionary definitions also include 'a: one that founds, supports, or inspires' and 'b: the leader of an organized crime syndicate.'

Interestingly in India (both in politics and Bollywood for that matter), the dictionary definition a: comes close and yet appears to enjoy a prominent status of its own.

SEEKING OUT THE GODFATHER

It all boils down to the above. Common party workers point out that for a successful career in Indian politics, the presence of a political godfather in one's life is a must. 'For any newcomer whose family has no connection whatsoever to politics, a godfather is a boon to have. But often the real task remains the ability to find one or be found by one,' opines an ageing grassroots worker on conditions of anonymity.

The Indian political landscape, which is largely dominated by dynastic politics, having a godfather by one's side does help to smooth out the difficult journey ahead which is mainly dominated by caste equations, money and muscle power, character assassinations and of course backbiting at its highest level. A typical godfather in Indian politics is someone who has access to lots of money, power and connections and the ability to 'get things done.'

Compared to the early seventies and eighties, almost all political parties in India today are overflowing with leaders controlling their camps of all castes and sizes, and these camps, in turn, continue to be dominated by 'self-proclaimed godfathers' who control their 'territory.' To seek out a godfather not only requires careful tact and skill but also the capability to identify whether the godfather is capable enough and has the necessary resources and aptitude to deliver on his promises from time to time.

While some foot soldiers may choose to be in the relationship with a godfather of their choice to gain foothold and positions in the party in the long run and even seek tickets for elections, others, despite sharing their deep loyalties with their godfather, may prefer to keep changing their political masters depending on the fortunes of the party that they are attached to.

In few cases though, those desirous to form permanent relationships with their godfathers opt for different routes such as marriage and business partnerships. By marrying into political families or families with affiliation to political entities ensures that the loyalties of the godfather stay with them a lifetime—irrespective of the fact whether their political careers take off or not. Since the human mind is fickle and more often easily attracted to all things materialistic, the lure of power and the perks that come attached to it aren't easy to let go. Many practise the art of social climbing, by ending up being stooges of the godfather to access that power and to bask in their glory. The affinity for upgraded social status is attractive and many find it easy to succumb to it too.

Yet another easy access to people already in positions of power and seeking out a godfather to groom their political ambitions is through the Indian Civil Services. There has been a long list of civil servants from the Indian Administrative Services (IAS), the Indian Foreign Services (IFS) and from the Indian Police Services (IPS) who have had fruitful beginnings in politics thanks to their political masters and associations with them.

The first example that comes to mind is that of veteran politician Yashwant Sinha. An IAS officer till 1984, he resigned from the service to join the Janata Party and was elected to the Rajya Sabha in 1988. He served as Finance Minister in 1990–91 and later on joined the BJP in 1996 where he was again appointed as Finance Minister and later as External Affairs Minister only to quit the party in 2018. Another few civil servants who have had illustrious careers in Indian politics are K. J. Alphone, a 1979 IAS batch officer who quit the services in 2006 to join politics or the 1968 batch IAS officer Ajit Jogi, who quit his job as a public servant to join the Congress Party holding several key positions including that of an MP as well. He later quit the Congress to form his party, the Janta Congress Chhattisgarh and became the first Chief Minister of Chhattisgarh in the year 2000. Or for that matter Jaya Prakash Narayana, from Andhra Pradesh who is considered to be one of the most popular IAS officer-turned-politician and has been controlling his own set of supporters too.

Or for that matter, Meira Kumar—the first woman to hold the position of Lok Sabha Speaker—she too hails from a Foreign Service background, where she served for over 10 years and headed the Social Justice and Empowerment portfolio under the Congress-led UPA government. Interestingly Kumar was nominated for the position of President by the party but lost out to the BJP candidate. And who can forget Meira's colleague, Natwar Singh who too, quit the foreign services to join the Congress party? Apart from heading the ministries of steel, coal mines and agriculture in the Rajiv Gandhi government, he also served as External Affairs Minister during the UPA government's tenure and was considered to be quite close to the Gandhi family. News reports suggest Singh, (the only leader to address the then Congress President Sonia Gandhi) fell from grace from the Gandhis' after his name was embroiled in the oil-for-food scandal that allegedly included his son Jagat.

Which brings us to the question as to what happens when one falls out with one's political mentor? Does this affect the relationship? Is loyalty above everything else?

UNDER THE GODFATHER'S SHADOW

Yet another Congress leader who claims to have fallen out of favour from his godfathers—the Gandhi family is none other than former IFS retiree, Mani Shankar Aiyar. The Lahore-born Aiyar, who joined the Indian Foreign Services in 1963, only to retire in 1989 and join politics under the mentorship of the late Rajiv Gandhi, recollects his journey and believes that loyalty to the godfather and his ideology is an ingredient evasive to the Indian political foot soldier.

Having held key positions in the government, the former Panchayati Raj minister believes that what you call loyalty is a very important quality to have in political life. He further adds that contrary to the fact, many people have made a political life out of disloyalty. 'So it is quite clear that whether you are loyal or disloyal, both of them in their ways have a role to play in building a political career. Some build a political career by defecting from one party to another, and others make a political career or lose a political career simply by sticking to their party and therefore I think I would evaluate the role of loyalty more in terms of personal ethics, then I would as a politically useful tool,' he states. There are some people for whom fidelity is part of their ethic of living and such people can find a future for themselves in politics. 'And I am perhaps a good example of both, the favourable political consequences of loyalty as well as the unfavourable consequences. Let me try and explain.'

He begins his story by saying that he had nothing in his background that was fit for a career in politics. 'My family are Tamil refugees from Pakistan so they are probably one of the smallest minorities in India. There was, therefore, no place anywhere. There was no money and there were no connections that would enable me to make my way into politics. Although the desire to be in politics had been aroused in me by the first general elections which I witnessed in 1952 at the age of 10 or 11. I was so enthused by that, that I organized an election in my class and imitated what the elders were doing. So, while I wanted more than anything else to be in politics I could see no way in which I could come in. Except that I was suddenly to my surprise inducted into the Prime Minister's office, when Rajiv Gandhi became the elected Prime Minister of India, in other words, I was not with him in the first two or three months. It was in February that I joined him and the time that I joined him I barely knew him. But in some ways, I could see that he knew me.'

Aiyar continues that this was because Rajiv was three years junior to him in school and when you are in a school for about five years, the senior person does not know the junior. But the junior person knows the senior. 'It is normal and natural. So, in a sense, he knew me and I had learnt that when I ran for President of the Union at Cambridge, Rajiv had gone around telling some Indian students, "There's an Indian running for President; at least you chaps can go there and vote." So, he began his political career by canvassing for me. Loyalty demands that I at my end began canvassing for him. And during the period that I was his joint secretary, I got to admire the man. Although there were several things on which he was faulted, and is still being faulted, I believe that he was a man of high integrity, high morality and that even if the consequences of being truthful and doing things according to his principles, was politically unfavourable, he nevertheless did it because it was the right thing to do.... And I admired this about him. So, then I realized because I was working with him on panchayati raj that this was my opportunity to come into politics. In August of 1989, I asked him for permission to resign from the foreign service. He was very reluctant. He said,

"You have a very good career ahead of you, why do you want to come into this wretched business of politics?"'

Aiyar recalls having said to him, 'I told him, "Well you have known ever since Cambridge that I am interested in being in politics, so please give me permission to resign from the service." So, many people think that he dragged me into politics. Indeed, for two months he wouldn't give me an answer and it was only after he had checked out in various ways, as to how serious I was or how sincere I was that eventually in early October 1989, he agreed that I could resign from the services and join him in politics.'

At that time, Aiyar reminisces that Rajiv told him that they would never make him a minister.

'I didn't ask why and instead said that it was fine with me. He didn't explain, he said not only Arun Singh but also Arun Nehru were not accepted by this system. So, you will not be accepted ... that is why I am reluctant, that you break a career in which you are doing well to come into the uncertainties of politics. I said, "I don't mind if you don't make me a minister, I want you to get me into Parliament." He said he would find a Rajya Sabha seat for me. But he was defeated in the election, and when he was defeated, he found that he really couldn't bring me into the Rajya Sabha despite his efforts and then the MP from Mayiladuthurai from Tamil Nadu a young man of 52 died of a diabetic seizure. So, when I saw from the papers that that seat had fallen vacant, I went to Rajiv and he was surprised that I was ready to fight the Lok Sabha elections, but then he backed me. So, I was helicoptered into my constituency, that brings me to the other question you asked about godfathers ... if Rajiv Gandhi had not helicoptered me into politics, there was no way that I could have made even a first entry.'

Aiyar continues that in return for his loyalty to him, which was being expressed in several articles he was writing, he was the one who offered him his patronage. 'I don't like the expression godfather, for that has criminal implications, but yes if it had not been for his patronage, I couldn't even have started on a political career,' he admits continuing that Rajiv's death changed it all. He was just about to return to office after a year's absence, and was on his way to his (Mani's) constituency to canvas for him. He was due to arrive in his constituency at 9.20 am the following morning but he got news of him being killed at 10.20 pm the previous evening.

LOSS OF PATRONAGE

'Post Rajiv's death, I had nobody to patronize me and nobody to pledge my loyalty to but I got elected. And when I got elected, I remained a Rajiv loyalist even though Narsimha Rao was the Prime Minister. Narsimha Rao didn't seem to mind this, although he was a little intrigued that I should continue to protest my loyalty to a dead man who was not going to be of political use for me. Especially so since Sonia Gandhi had refused to enter even public life let alone political life and stuck to her stand for nearly 8 years,' he says further adding, 'What I discovered was that although she was not in public or political life, she was generally keeping her hand on my shoulder; therefore, the professional politicians like Narsimha Rao understood that if they were to act against my interest, she may well either reprimand them or appraise them or at any rate come to my assistance. There was, in fact, a case where a disciplinary case was instituted against me. She was abroad. She was in fact in Kazakhstan, and from Almaty, where she discovered that this disciplinary case against me had been instituted. She telephoned and told Mr Narsimha Rao, that you can't proceed against him like this. So, although it was not very overt and not very obvious, Sonia Gandhi picked up that patronage after her husband passed away. And I enjoyed her patronage without even knowing it for the six or seven years from 1991 till the end of 1997 when she was not in politics and was refusing to come into politics.'

In the December of 1997, he confesses, he had strong differences with Mr Sitaram Kesari, because he had sent Vijaybhaskar Reddy as his representative to meet Jayalalitha and work out the terms of the Congress alliance with the AIADMK. And the latter had told Vijay Bhaskar that unless Kesari came and met her the next day she was going to join the BJP. 'So when Vijay Bhaskar told me this on the phone, I rushed to Mr Kesari and tried to persuade him to leave immediately for Chennai and he said, "Why should we go to South India, we first have to fix up things in North India." And I said that this was not the attitude that a Congress leader should have—this country is one and the South matters as much as the North. So, I was very upset and I left the party. And at that time, Mamata Banerjee too left the Congress for her reasons as she was also upset at that time. And she asked me to join her newly formed Trinamool Congress and I agreed to join her. But after I had been with the new Trinamool Congress for three weeks or so, I found that it was a very regional party; it was not oriented towards national politics and I felt very out of place there, so, although she had found for me the constituency of Barrackpore and after the elections were over told me that I could have easily won there, I didn't feel comfortable being in a regional party and so I took my leave and went to my constituency which I contested as an independent against the official Congress candidate. But soon after the elections in March of 1998, Sonia Gandhi would come into the Congress around 30 or 31 December to pour over the resolution of the party. And I had met her and told her that as soon as she became the President of the party, I would return to the Congress.'

Aiyar says that he returned to the Congress, but there were many people in the Congress, the top leaders who said that the Congress rules are that anybody who contests against a Congressman would have to remain out of the party for six years. Sonia Gandhi overruled them and enabled him to come back to the party and she gave him a lot of attention and care. 'So that silent patronage which had been there ever since her husband died became overt once she became the President of the Congress party. I returned her patronage by being loyal to her. So it went both ways—loyalty as well as patronage. And then I was unexpectedly rewarded. When nobody, not even Manmohan Singh wanted to make me a minister, or a Cabinet minister, it was because of Sonia's insistence that I should be India's first-ever Union Panchayati Raj minister. I remember I told her that as Union Panchayati Raj minister (as Panchayati Raj is a state subject) I would only be able to push matters unless I was able to interact with a Chief Minister, and interaction with a Chief Minister would be possible only if I were a Cabinet Minister. So, I was made a Cabinet Minister. I wouldn't have been ever made a Cabinet Minister and that too with so many portfolios had it not been for Sonia Gandhi. So, that patronage worked very well for me,' he admits.

After he lost in the elections of 2009, Aiyar says that within a couple of months Sonia Gandhi found him a sinecure, the position of an Honorary Advisor. That was the title of the Bureau of Parliamentary Studies and Training which entitled him to a nice big home in Lutyen's Delhi. In a few months after that, she got him nominated as the President's nominee to the Rajya Sabha.

'And I had a full six years as a member of the Rajya Sabha making my political career a total of 21 years. Fifteen years in three terms in the Lok Sabha and six years in the Rajya Sabha; but, it was about the time that she made me a member of the Rajya Sabha that she lost her trust in me. So, I never got a political position in the party although I was in the Rajya Sabha. It is only in the last 10 years that I have lost her confidence,' he says confessing that he is not even able to get an appointment to see her.

Why did she lose her trust?

'Well, there was one incident that involved Mr Chidambaram where I was misunderstood but I was never allowed to explain and so although I was a member of the Rajya Sabha and given certain special assignments on subjects that I had worked with Rajiv Gandhi, the party had not expressed any great interest. This included disarmament, zonal cultural centres, and panchayati raj and gave me special assignments, and at the end of that period for a year I was given Cabinet rank. So, while her patronage remained, it was all in a distant cold sense. There was a complete absence of any personal contact with her,' Aiyar says.

Aiyar believes that the party may have been jealous of his professional relationship with her and that he was no longer in touch with her soon became obvious to other party members as well.

'They took a long time to discover it. I, of course, recognized it immediately. But everyone in the party only learnt of it slowly when they found that I was not being given any political position in the party, I was not being allowed to speak to her at all in the India Congress Committee meeting. So, with the loss of that patronage, I also found myself being sidelined by other senior leaders in the party. Nobody was ready to speak up for me. And some of my friends who are amongst the senior people and had talked to her said to me that there was something wrong. But they didn't tell me what it was. And Mrs Gandhi is a rather reticent lady, so she doesn't explain but anyway the fact of the matter is that I lost out. And then in the last two or three years, I have also been ignored by Rahul Gandhi. And I have had one meeting with Priyanka Gandhi but that's it. I know that I have lost the patronage of the Gandhi family and therefore I am not going to ever again get any position of any significance.'

He says that this leads a lot of people to ask him as to why does he not leave the party. To which he replies, 'Well that's where my loyalty comes. My loyalty is also to certain principles, to a certain philosophy, to a certain political stance, and I remain what I have always been through my life, a Nehruvian socialist in a Nehruvian circumference. I am more a follower of the Congress ideology and its principles than merely being a follower of the Gandhi family. It is because of the patronage of the Gandhi family that I have been able to find a position in the party and when that patronage was withdrawn I lost that position but that did not lead to my leaving the party or wanting to leave the party. Because my higher loyalty is to the ideology of the party and it is explained by the fact that I was six years old when Nehru became the Prime Minister of India and I was 23 years old when he died. So, for the 17 formative years of my life, Nehru was a colossal figure bestriding this nation. I have always been a strong Nehruvian and I enjoyed a special relationship with Rajiv Gandhi because we were about the same age. I was never, in those terms, close to Sonia but she extended me her patronage. That is why, under her, I was able to repeatedly come back to parliament and become a minister. I am very grateful to her and her husband for their patronage, and to Nehru for forming my mind and almost all the beliefs that I had. But I think, in the end, loyalty to an idea must prevail over loyalty to a person. I don't think I was ever loyal to a person. I was loyal to persons who embodied that philosophy and who were able to carry that philosophy forward. So, I would say that my loyalty was not to an individual but to a political ideology and those who represented it and those who made good of it. But my loyalty was essentially to those principals and that philosophy and not to personalities,' he trails off.

●●● ──────────── ●●●

What happens when the ones who have brought you up take away that privilege from you? What happens when your mentor gives up on you? Former Congress Minister, Mani Shankar Aiyar's remarkably opens up to share his story of the consequences that follow when one's godfather is no more and political patronage is lost. Aiyar's disclosure of the treatment meted out to him by his colleagues post his fallout with the Gandhi family is an eye-opener in itself. While many foot soldiers did confess that having a godfather is a crucial element in one's political career, many others also believed that attaching oneself to the mercy of any particular family or person/mentor can be a deterrent in the long run as well. Especially in cases, where the godfather or mentor's fortunes tend to be on a decline, those close to him or in his circle run the risk of becoming the first victims as they tend to be easily targeted. Hence it often helps to leave one's options open and rely only on one's good sense and ability than depend on the whims and fancies of a godfather to further one's fortunes.

6 The Money Rota

For any political party to function smoothly, the availability of resources like manpower and funds remain an all-important factor. The need is even more crucial during election periods.

More than manpower, funds top the list of priorities and political parties are known to make use of their workers well to generate funds to keep the party machinery running smoothly. A party flush with funds can not only successfully manoeuvre itself through difficult situations but can also take care of its workers well and survive in the long run. While seeking donations during rallies or through relief funds is one of the ways funding is sought, there are many untraditional methods of generating money which have been open to criticism as well. Although the most popular methods of raising funds remain through individuals, public and corporates, most political parties fail to divulge the actual sources of their funding even today.

Unions are one of the key sources of funding for a political party, and a party that controls more number of unions not only has control over the people attached to it but also over the funds that it generates. The reign of the Communist Party in Mumbai in the late sixties and seventies declined only after its unions comprising largely of mill workers were decimated following the mill workers strike. The strike which continues to exist on paper even today led to a large number of workers shifting their affiliations to other political parties such as the newly formed Shiv Sena led by its founder Balasaheb Thackeray.

Eighty-two-year-old Madan Yeshwant Naik from the CPI (M) recalls that his party even today has several trade unions which contribute to the funding of the party through its many trade union *shakhas*. For example, there is the Mumbai Shramik Sangh, Engineering Workers Union, Anganwadi Union, Ghar Kamgar Union, including the Bhadekaru Kriti Samiti to name a few. From the trade unions, full-time workers at various offices receive an honorarium for giving their time and also for other expenses, including funding for elections. During elections, the party, he says, also raises election funds by printings coupons of different denominations of ₹10 onwards. They print blank coupons books too. Apart from that, those desirous of contributing can still contribute.

Although parties do not feel it is important to divulge their sources of funding, for public knowledge, one of the most common ways of generating funds for any political party is through its membership drives wherein workers resort from door-to-door or face-to-face campaigning to enroll supporters of the party or leadership asking them to pledge their services for a fee. These fees may range anywhere from as low as ₹5 to over ₹150 per person, depending on the amount the party leadership decides. And workers enrolling the largest number of members and generating considerable amounts in funding may get adequately rewarded for their efforts either through promotions or merely being felicitated at public party functions to boost their morale.

Over the years, political parties, to attract funding from all avenues have taken to forming 'cells' such as the IT cell to attract those from the IT sector, the corporate cell to attract membership as well as funding from the corporate sector, regional cells concentrated specifically towards attracting funding from states (the BJP, for instance, has a Bihar cell to attract entrepreneurs and workers from Bihar), etc. Interestingly, appointments for key positions within parties are also considered keeping in mind not only the caste factor of the candidate but also his ability to generate funds for the party. For instance, a certain national political party is always known to appoint its party presidents who belong to the business community for them to get access to easy and quick funding whenever needed especially during elections.

As per Association for Democratic Reforms (ADR) and several news reports between 2004–05 and 2018–19, national political parties have collected around ₹11,234.12 crores from unknown sources (2020). The report further states that during 2018–19, the BJP declared ₹1,612.04 crores as income from unknown sources which is 64 per cent of the total income of National Parties from unknown sources (₹2,512.98 crores). 'This income of BJP forms more than 1.5 times the aggregate of income from unknown sources declared by the other five National Parties (₹900.94 crores)' (ADR report).

The report further informs that out of ₹2,512.98 crores as income from unknown sources, the share of income from Electoral Bonds was ₹1,960.68 crores or 78 per cent of the amount. The report reads,

> The combined income of INC and NCP from the sale of coupons between FY 2004–05 and 2018–19 stands at ₹3,902.63 crores. According to the donation reports (containing details of donations above ₹20,000) of FY 2018–19, ₹71.44 lakhs was given to the National Parties by cash. For this report, known sources have been defined as donations above ₹20,000, whose donor details are available through contributions report as submitted by National parties to the Election Commission of India (ECI). The unknown sources are income declared in the IT returns but without giving a source of income for donations below ₹20,000. Such unknown sources include 'donations via Electoral Bonds', 'sale of coupons', 'relief fund', 'miscellaneous income', 'voluntary contributions', 'contribution from meetings/morchas', etc. The details of donors of such voluntary contributions are not available in the public domain. Other known sources of income include the

sale of moveable & immoveable assets, old newspapers, membership fees, delegate fees, bank interest, sale of publications, and levy whose details would be available in the books of accounts maintained by political parties.

For this analysis, seven national parties had been considered—BJP, INC, AITC, CPM, NCP, BSP and CPI.

However, BSP declared that it did not receive any funds from voluntary contributions (above or below ₹20,000) / Sale of Coupons / Electoral Bonds or Unknown Sources of income. Total income of 7 National political parties in FY 2018–19: ₹3,749.37 crores. Total income of political parties from known donors (details of donors as available from contribution report submitted by parties to Election Commission and analysed by ADR here): ₹951.66 crores, which is 25.38 per cent of the total income of the parties. Total income of political parties from other known sources (e.g. sale of assets, membership fees, bank interest, sale of publications, party levy, etc.): ₹284.73 crores, or 7.59 per cent of the total income. Total income of political parties from unknown sources (income specified in the IT Returns whose sources are unknown): ₹2,512.98 crores, which is 67% of the total income of the parties. Out of ₹2,512.98 crores as income from unknown sources, the share of income from Electoral Bonds: ₹1,960.68 crores or 78 per cent. Out of total income of ₹2,512.98 crores of 6 National Parties from unknown sources, 78.02 per cent or ₹1960.68 crores came from Electoral Bonds.

THE JOURNEY OF POLITICAL FUNDRAISING

Party workers who not only manage to raise maximum funds but also run successful campaigns to keep their party running, rise high within the ranks and are considered to be important assets by their party leadership.

One such story is that of Arvind Ganpat Sawant, from the Shiv Sena. The 60-year-old veteran party leader is credited for setting up a union for the employees of the Mahanagar Telephone Nigam Limited and Maharashtra State Road Transport—two most important unions which to this date, remain the most influential of all unions in Mumbai/Maharashtra as they have a large number of memberships through their employees. Arvind goes down memory lane explaining that the Shiv Sena never gave money to work for them. The (MP) states that they have had to raise our own money to run the party. 'It was important to be inspired by thoughts and ideology and work towards that. You don't need money for all of these things. You do it (raise funds) out of loyalty and dedication to the party,' he states.

I am seated in his office-cum-*shakha* in Parel to interview him for this book. It is a Saturday and the politician, although having given me an appointment, is nowhere to be seen. After enquiring with Sawant telephone for his absence, he tells me to come after two hours as he had to rush to the hospital for an emergency case for his assistance. But I insist on waiting to not miss him again. While we do meet briefly for a few minutes, we part ways only to resume our interview for the second time at his other office at Shivaji Park in Dadar. The wait at both of Sawant's offices proved to be worthwhile. It gave me a chance to see his staff in action even while the leader himself wasn't present where things appeared to move smoothly.

Arvind is one of the oldest party members of the Shiv Sena—a two-time Member of Legislative Council (MLC) and a first time MP from South Mumbai, a seat earlier controlled by the Congress for decades. Although a leader in his own right, Arvind's story is one of the most crucial ones in understanding as to why in an age where political loyalties amongst party workers are short-lived, he continues to be one of the oldest and most dedicated supporters of not only the party but also its current leadership and warmly shares his story.

THE COMMENCEMENT

'Shiv Sena, since its birth, had the blessings of artists, who painted the walls with beautiful handwriting and jingles, such as *Thamb Laxmi Kunku Lavate, Shivsenela Mat Devun yete*, which means, 'wait Laxmi, I will come back to adorn you with sindoor, only after I have given my vote to Shivsena during elections'. I was the one who loved and did these writings on Shiv Sena's boards and walls. And the most important were the great speeches, cartoons and editorials of our beloved leader Shri Balasaheb Thackeray with his heart-touching vocabulary that inspired almost everyone from young to old to join the party. I remember when the Shiv Sena was first set up—I came to know of it through the weekly Marathi magazine *Marmik* that Balasaheb used to edit. I also used to read a Marathi daily called *Navashakti*. Those were my school days. In Shirodkar High School, Parel where I used to study, talented students were provided room for extra studies and I was one of them. In 1968, the municipal corporation elections for Mumbai were in the offing. Congress had planned a meeting in the school auditorium. At that time, a pair of bullocks tied to the yoke was the election symbol of the Congress party and this was installed at the main gate of the hall of my high school,' he recalls. It had been unbearable for him to digest this and he, along with three to four students, had shouted Shiv Sena slogans for which they had been punished by their teacher with a rope stick. 'Every hit and wound of the rope stick made my in-built Shiv Sainik more poignant and stronger,' he states.

The *chowk sabha*s and direct meetings were the major means of campaigning in that era. Easy means of communication, television network or social media did not exist. In those times, *chowk sabha*s or corner meetings were generally conducted by all the political parties to reach out to the public. And many parties used to use jingles to reach out to us. Arvind, recalls how he used to chant Shiv Sena's most famous song, '*Vijayashrichi maal kunala? Ugach ka ho karata vaad? Thayi thayi ghosh ek, Shiv Sena Zindabad, Shiv Sena Zindabad.*' (Who will be entitled to the garland of victory? Why are you making an argument over this? Every footstep has a single voice, that Shiv Sena will be victorious.)

'During that election, Hon'ble Shri Balasaheb allied with PSP (Praja Samajwadi Party). Barrister Nath Pai, S. M. Joshi, N. G. Gore, Madhu Dandavate were leaders of that party. At that time, the Rashtra Seva Dal was one of the cultural wings of PSP. They used to sing satirical songs against the then rulers of Brihanmumbai Municipal Corporation (BMC) and the state of Maharashtra. Shahir Sabaleji brought satirical drama, which inspired Marathi people to strengthen the Shiv Sena.'

He recalls how the Marathi people were enthralled and inspired by *Marmik's* articles in series like *'Vaacha ani thand basa' 'Agralekh'*, *'Kunchala', 'Jatra'* (Read only, Don't react, Editorial, Brush Strokes, and cartoons named as 'Ravivarchi Jatra' etc). 'The Marathi people,' he says, 'were inspired by reading these articles and agonized by the injustice they faced.' To understand the Sena, one must travel back to the sixties when the state of Maharashtra was formed and 106 martyrs had sacrificed their lives for undivided Maharashtra. Arvind believes that despite the division, Marathi people did not get their due share in employment opportunities in Mumbai. In 1969, Shiv Sena sacrificed 69 veterans for Marathi people residing in the regions of Belgaum, Karwar, Dharwad, Nipani, Bhalki and Bidar areas which are present in the state of Karnataka. He recollects the vibrant speech made by the Shiv Sena *pramukh* at Trikoni Maidan (now known as Sadakant Dhavan Maidan) in Naigaon, which enthralled the Marathi people. He was actively involved in the movement started thereafter and even endured brutal beatings at the hands of the police to break down the protest. This, he says, made him an even stronger and determined Shiv Sainik.

'It was obvious to be expected by all that there would be the rule of Marathi-speaking people here. At that time, the Congress party was a prominent power in the state,' he continues further adding that the *Marmik* used to publish a list of names of the people employed in both public and private sector companies like banks and other organizations. Interestingly, the list did not have a single

Marathi name featured in it. The feature was introduced in the magazine to raise the question as to where was the Marathi *manus* for whom the state had been founded?

The Communist Party was a little powerful, as they led many trade unions in Mumbai around that time (they were prominent in Sewri where Arvind used to stay) as well as in entire Girgaum. He believes their struggle was a complicated one as they kept their workers and people within strict boundaries, within fences.

Arvind adds that although large parts of Mumbai were under the stronghold of socialist thought and ideology, they lacked emotional connect. 'The plight of the Marathi *manus* (man) was missing from their narrative which was why Maharashtrians could connect with the Shiv Sena and Balasaheb Thackeray's clarion call of sons-of-the-soil movement easily. It was the movement of the right to have bread, the right to have a job to earn that bread for the family. The Shiv Sena identified the basic need of the Maharashtrians—*naukri, bhakri* and *asmita* (job, food and respect). A lot many locals were struggling to get these basic things in their daily lives,' he adds.

Arvind points out that many times, he has experienced that his great patriot leader Balasaheb was misunderstood, misquoted and misinterpreted. 'He was a lion-hearted man! He never discriminated anyone by caste, creed and religion. You must realize that a lot of Maharashtrians were struggling to get food, jobs, and the self-respect and dignity that they deserved. Initially, Balasaheb wanted to start an organization that would only work for the benefit of the Marathi *manus* and their cause. He wasn't very keen on getting involved in the politics of contesting elections. But later, he thought and realized that without power he would not be able to deliver good for the society and Marathi *manus*. Hence, he decided to contest the elections. He used to say "Power is not my goal but it is a weapon used to achieve the goal of service to the common man". Balasaheb always said and I quote his words, "*Brahman brahmanyetar, Maratha-marathyetar,*

96 kuli, 92 kuli, uccha neech, Dalit, dalitetar, sprushya asprushya, ghati-kokani he saare bheda galun Marathi manasa ek ho. Tar aani tarach tula nyay milel." (Brahmans, Marathas, Dalits, touchables, untouchables, etc., only if you come together and unite as one Marathi you can get justice.) Social work should be perseverance. The other was to bury the hatchets such as Brahmin–non-Brahmin, Maratha–non-Maratha, Ghati–Konkani, Dalit–non-Dalit, touchables–untouchables and that of casteism and stand united as Marathi for Maharashtra. Unknowingly, the foundation of the Shiv Sena was founded based on this social work that the *shakha*s were doing. The Shiv Sena *pramukh* gave two major ideologies for the party to follow i.e. 80 per cent social work and 20 per cent politics. Based on these ideologies, *shakha*s were established at the grassroots level to provide justice to the aggrieved, to provide relief to those in grief, to give rights to all. They were not just *shakha*s, but they were temples of justice. Whether it was school admission, a family issue or the health of senior family members or women safety, Shiv Sena used to offer a helping hand to anyone who was aggrieved. With this relentless social work, Shiv Sena grew further. For more than five decades now, Shiv Sena has been organizing blood donation camps, health consultation camps, ophthalmic camps, cleanliness drives which have helped it to grow among the masses. Through its blood donation drive, Shiv Sena created a Guinness Book of World Record by collecting more than 25,000 bottles of blood on a single day.'

Today, he claims, we see, so many cleanliness drives being run as publicity campaigns, but the Shiv Sena *pramukh* was the first to have initiated these cleanliness drives in those days. 'The Shiv Sainiks used to clean the garbage from dirty rail tracks and even the lanes. I recollect the then Shiv Sena Leader Hon'ble Shri Wamanrao Mahadik, who was also former Mayor and MLA had built two-storied public toilets at Shiv Sena Nagari, Naigaon and Bhoiwada and thereafter it became a trend to provide for public toilets. One of the major and most popular activities of the party was to provide free ambulance service for the public which was available at every *shakha*. Handing over an ambulance for public usage was first initiated by Shiv Sena at Girgaum. The Shiv Sena *pramukh* instructed to make available the ambulance in all the *shakhas* (branches) and the party has been doing this social work irrespective of victory or defeat, position or power calculations. The party continued such social work for the past five decades and hence flourished at the grassroots level.'

He claims that while doing this, there was no basis for caste discrimination then and neither is it there now. 'You could be a Gujarati or a Muslim or any other but a Marathi first—that was all that mattered. In the *shakhas*, we never asked anybody their caste or their backgrounds. Even now, no one asks for them. We used to have *shakha pramukhs* from minority backgrounds back in 1968. It is a wrong notion that the Shiv Sena is against Muslims. Even in the seventies, our zilla *pramukhs* were Muslims. They were actively involved with us and our movement for the Marathi *manus*. The late Shri Shabir Shaikh was zilla *pramukh* of Thane district and who later became the minister during the Shiv Sena–BJP regime in Maharashtra.'

Saheb, he continues, never enquired about the caste of anyone, not until caste reservations were introduced in elections. 'He felt pained to even enquire about their background especially and when he had to nominate people according to caste, he used to feel very bad about it.' He claims that the Shiv Sena had no offices of its own when it first started and people had begun approaching them in large numbers for help. They ended up meeting and listening to their woes mostly on the playgrounds or the gymnasiums where they used to sit as they were open for the public free of charge. Now, he says, every inch of space in Mumbai is up for sale. 'In due course, few benefactors began donating their own spaces to set up our *shakhas*. At that time, there wasn't too much illegal construction like there is now. You would be surprised to know that even the police stations began advising people who used to come to complain to them on local issues to visit the *shakhas* for solutions to their problems.'

The *shakha*, in itself, was a court of justice. They solved a lot of problems—people then did not even approach their local MLAs or corporators, but them instead, knowing that their work would surely be done. So, from petty household fights to cleaning the garbage on the streets, to providing affordable kerosene to people who could not afford it, Arvind says, he did all of that. 'These *shakhas* used to operate on donations. People used to donate part of their salaries on running them. A lot of people helped us in kind and not in cash. No one kept a bank account then to see who was spending on what. Soon other parties began to feel threatened with the kind of politics, with the thought and movement of the Sena, and they began troubling us. They tried all the tricks in their books to put down the work by the Sena. In the beginning, around 1966–78, we were badly beaten up by the police. To shut down this movement for the Marathi *manus*, the Congress party which was in power at that time, made full use of the police in the Home Department to beat up the Sainiks and shut down the party forever. Many have died in police custody then. But that did not deter us. Instead, it made us much stronger,' he recalls.

In 1968, the Shiv Sena had a tie-up with the Praja Samajwadi Party. And in that election, the party got its first 42 corporators elected for BMC. This was a boost to the workers who had sacrificed a lot for the party. 'I can proudly say that the Shiv Sena is one party where loyalists are highest in number compared to any other party in the country. They do not aim for personal achievements, their only aim has always been working for the success of the party alone,' Arvind states with pride going down memory lane adding that there were many ups and downs in the political scene at that time. 'The Janta Dal party, for instance, was a buzz at one time in 1977, but no Sainiks went there. They remained loyal to Balasaheb alone. He had predicted that the Janta Dal won't last for long, and his words proved true with time. I failed to understand, from where he had got this perfect prediction, the ability to read the future. Maybe him being a cartoonist, he had a quality to 'read between the lines' which was reflected in his political predictions.'

LOKADHIKAR AND THE SHIV SENA

Arvind still remembers the historic and massive movement for the rights of the Marathi people and the sons of the soil. The Shiv Sena *pramukh*, he states, established the *sthaniya lokadhikar samiti* in all the organizations to make more efforts in a disciplined manner to provide job opportunities and to extend the rights to the sons of the soil on a priority basis. The marching of the *sthaniya lokadhikar samiti*, who strived hard to deliver justice to the Marathi people, started through the organizations in Mumbai offices on a fast-track basis. The *sthaniya lokadhikar samiti* was the only organization whose activists never cared for their jobs but cared more to deliver justice to the masses.

'In those days, a board announcing the vacancies in government/private jobs/PSU jobs used to be put up outside every *shakha* to update the Marathi youth on the various job openings. We noticed that most of our Marathi boys and girls lacked the education or the expertise to apply for these positions and hence through the *sthaniya lokadhikar samiti*, we began introducing free training classes for them. We began giving training for written tests. The boys were prepared on what kind of questions would be asked during interviews and mind you, this training continues even today. I am proud to say that over the years the party has groomed lakhs of young boys and girls for government and private jobs. The *sthaniya lokadhikar samiti* made a major impact. Any work started by the Sena—whether it is the local employment drive, food distribution, ambulance services, tree plantation or blood donation drive, health camps for one and all—has never been temporary or done only keeping elections in mind; the Sena, even today, continues to do that work irrespective of the consequences.'

Meanwhile, along with his involvement in these social activities in his personal life, Arvind in 1976 got a job at Bombay Telephones (as it was called then) where he took the initiative in the *sthaniya lokadhikar samiti* to push for recruitment of Maharashtrians in Bombay Telephones which had become MTNL in April 1986.

'I still remember, in the year 1986, the MTNL announced a recruitment drive for 350 junior engineers through advertisements in the papers. All the 350 candidates for the posts, who were selected were not only from out of the town of Mumbai but also out of Maharashtra. There was not a single Maharashtrian domicile in the list of 350 applicants. I protested against this. I said that I would not allow a single applicant from outside Maharashtra to be recruited. Does this mean that not a single candidate is eligible from entire Maharashtra? Under the Employment Exchange Act, the unemployed youth of all categories register their names at the regional Employment Exchanges. The companies that need to hire candidates send their requirements to these employment exchanges and, in turn, receive resumes with the requisite qualifications, age, experience, in the ratio of 1:10; the companies, then, select the required candidates from them. I found that nothing was followed by MTNL as per this Act. The candidates were selected without any written test and interview. We, under the banner of the *sthaniya lokadhikar samiti*, carried the agitation and demanded that the sons of the soil should be given preference. The most shocking information we received in the University of Madras and some other universities of the South was that if you have passed any examination of graduation and did not achieve the desired marks or class in the examination, you are allowed to reappear for the same examination to improve your performances. I found that some candidates were selected on the merit of their marks in such examinations which was an injustice to other candidates who do not get such opportunities. Moreover, it was again a violation of the Employment Exchange Act. Hence, a lot many people were taking advantage of this and were coming to Mumbai to get jobs. And our Marathi students (there used to be a handful of them who secured 1st Class in the BSc or engineering examinations) often ended at the bottom of the merit list so that they were not even considered for selection. Moreover, there was no written test, no interview, so they did not have any opportunity to prove their credentials.' The management, accepting their basic mistake, carried the fresh recruitment as per law by which all 350 juniors engineers got selected from the sons of the soil. During his protest, Arvind says, the police had surrounded him and were about to arrest him too. 'During the agitation, we had blocked the entire Veer Sawarkar Road, which is a VVIP Road, at Prabhadevi.'

In the year 1984–85, when Arvind passed the departmental examination for the post of Junior Engineer, he was sent for training to the centre at Madras for a year. When he reached there, he experienced that the people of Madras were very 'regionalistic' and were not ready to respond in either Hindi or any other language except in a little bit of English. So was the mentality of the staff at the training centre. 'In our hostel, we had a television. Those were the days of Doordarshan which used to telecast the news in the regional language at 8 p.m., in the national language of Hindi at 9 p.m. and English at 10 p.m. In Tamil Nadu, there were restrictions on Hindi news. The state government had officially disallowed Hindi news to be shown. To add to our grievance of not understanding the language, the warden of the hostel used to switch off the TV often at 9 p.m. I requested him to keep the sports room open till the English news at 10 p.m. was over, but he did not respond positively. Immediately, I remembered my Shiv Sena and Shiv Sena *pramukh* and how they did not allow me to keep quiet. Our *pramukh* never inculcated hatred in us for any language or people. He insisted that the language and people of a state should be honoured. He always demanded preference for the sons of the soil in which there were so many other communities involved and who were born and brought up for generations together in Maharashtra. Hence, I revolted against this decision about switching off the TV without listening to the news in a language we understood. . . . Although we were working in the communication department, we were deprived of any communication, especially news, and that was irritating. Due to my agitation, they finally agreed to keep the sports room open till 10.30 p.m. My entire batch of trainees along with the trainees of other states congratulated me.'

Due to this protest, the trainees elected Arvind as the Secretary of the Sports Committee. Since he always stood first in his training, post his protest, his marks were cut citing indiscipline. But Arvind claims he stood his ground and won.

Food was another problem. On all days they were served *sambar, mor* (buttermilk), rice, *idli*s and no vegetables. 'We got fed up with this monotonous food system. I demanded *chapati*s, and for this too, we fought and finally got *chapati*s and even *paratha*s. I used to work for the *sanghatana* while doing my job. The telecom field was also going through a revamp and although MTNL was expanding, its employees were neglected.'

He claims that while experiencing all of this, he realized the importance of the need of unions and on his return to Mumbai, with the blessings of *vandaniya* Balasaheb and through the *sthaniya lokadhikar samiti*, in 1988, he took the step ahead proactively and founded a union in MTNL. 'I visited 150 offices personally to explain the working of the *samiti* to its employees. After establishing the union, I revisited the 150 offices and took gate meetings to explain the vision and mission of the union and got the rest of the unions with mutual understanding under the umbrella of the Mahanagar Telephone Nigam Kamgar Sangh and got it registered.'

Another union was active at Delhi during the same period. In collaboration with that union, they held a token strike in 1990 which was a tremendous success. The government declared on the spot a salary increment of ₹100 temporarily and agreed to consider all demands positively. 'This union set up by us and even when it wasn't a recognized one has created history. We compelled the Union Government to decide about the fate and status of MTNL employees since they were neither treated as government servants nor as employees of the Public Sector Unit (PSU) and hence were deprived of their legitimate pay and perks as per those of the PSU employees. Our union carried agitations for 12 years and eventually was successful. A historical wage agreement was made at that time. Before that, an election was carried by MTNL to decide the majority union to negotiate the salary and perks with the management. Our 'Kamgar Sangh' contested the election and won by achieving more than 72 per cent votes. Balasaheb was so happy at that time that he congratulated and blessed us. I cannot forget that day. MTNL is the only one that has provided the best of facilities for its members. I never had to call a strike ever. There were numerous *andolan*s but the decision to go on strike was taken only once in my entire career of 30 years in the form of a one-day "tool down, pen down". Over the years, I have managed to get all my demands for employees accepted without any fight, tussles, etc., while keeping in mind the interest of the company.'

Arvind adds that his leader always said that it was okay to do *andolan*s and stage protests but they should be accompanied by solutions as well which was why he always went with solutions and these solutions could never be rejected by anyone as they were practical ones. He claims that his leader inculcated in them a very great thought that if the company survived, then employees too would survive. 'With these thoughts in my mind, I led the union. Not only did I form the trade union for the employees of MTNL but also with our *sthaniya lokadhikar samiti*, we started doing a lot of social activities from the funds of the union for our employees as well as for the society. We launched the programme for facilitating the education of the children of our employees, who secured more than 80 per cent marks in SSC examinations as well as those who showed excellence in any field. We held blood donation camps, received appreciation from the KEM Hospital Blood Bank for highest blood donations, carried health check-up camps for our female employees and formed Mahila Kalyan Samitis to protect the interest of female employees.'

But it was the sons-of-the-soil movement that changed everything. The people, he says, working for this movement had full-time jobs; yet they risked those very jobs and fought with their management to recruit locals—people whom they did not know or weren't their relatives at all. A lot of them faced suspension from their management, many more lost their jobs while there was disciplinary action against some, but Arvind claims that his movement did not stop. 'The management of many companies were wary of us and gave in when we went to meet them saying *'nahi nahi jhagada nahi karna hain'*. Ours was a legitimate demand—that of giving jobs to local people first rather than to migrants. Today, every other party and leader is copying this. Look at Shri Yogi Adityanath, the Hon'ble Chief Minister of Uttar Pradesh. He recently said he would see to it that locals get jobs in Uttar Pradesh. Earlier, many used to criticize us. The great beloved leader Hon'ble Shri Balasaheb had said the same thing. He never said give 100 per cent jobs to locals but always said at least give 80 per cent of it. We are not talking about skilled jobs. That is a different case altogether. I cannot ask someone who cannot drive well to be selected as a driver, which is a skilled job. But if there are more than two or three drivers and one of them belongs to Maharashtra, who is efficient, he should be given first preference. Our needs were legitimate and within the framework of the law. So much so that at that time, leading Marathi newspapers like *Loksatta* and *Navakaal* supported our protests through their articles and editorials.'

From campaigning, the topic now shifts to the 1993 Mumbai riots wherein the Shiv Sena was known to have played a role. Arvind, when questioned on the same, says, 'Let me be very open on the subject. Shiv Sena is not an action but a reaction! The constitution gives me the right to protect my life. If I try to attack you now, will you keep quiet? I am sure you will not. We did not burn Radhabai Chawl (the first incident of a communal riot where some Hindu families were burnt in a chawl in Jogeshwari that sparked off the Mumbai riots). The fact was that 40 people were locked in that chawl and burnt alive, no one protested about that and till date, no one speaks about it except Hon'ble Balasaheb. Even during Gujarat riots, I remember saheb had asked, "Why do they keep quiet about Godhra? Gujarat riots were a reaction to the Godhra incident." Where was the government at that time? What were they doing? Were they waiting for rioters to come on the streets to kill more people? Tell me one incident where the Shiv Sena has done an *andolan* (protest) and went on a rampage beating up people for no reason. We believe in 100 per cent social work and to stand for the *rashtra* (nation) first and then Maharashtra.'

During all this time, he claims his family's support has been immense. 'It is my good fortune that my wife too was an employee of MTNL. Ours is an arranged marriage. Many a time, I have had to miss out on important occasions, like the birth of my son, due to party work. My family was very religious to some extent and that had an impact on me. They used to follow the saints and their sayings and that has had an impact on me from a very young age. But the biggest god for me was the Shiv Sena *pramukh* himself! He was so giving, he never kept anything for himself. For someone like him, who only gives, how can we keep something for ourselves? Why should we keep expectations? Our generation has always followed such thinking, if we get something in return for what we do, fine, if not, then too there is no regret.'

Balasaheb, he says, changed the lives of many people. Common people were made corporators, MLAs and even ministers. Some went on to even higher positions. He believes, he too was fortunate to be noticed by saheb. 'There were many others too, but I will always be indebted to him that he gave me an opportunity. I know of many people who want to get ahead in life soon and end up frustrated if they don't. I took a long time to get here but I have no regrets. I am not politically ambitious. I never get sleepless nights thinking that I have to become so and so. I am so tired that at the end of the day when I lie on my bed, sleep comes to me immediately. I don't worry much. I have been granted an opportunity by the beloved Balasaheb and Hon'ble Uddhav*ji* to serve the people, Maharashtra and the *rashtra*, which I should do loyally and dedicatedly which I have been and am doing sincerely and honestly. I have no problems with either success or failure because I believe I have been born a Shiv Sainik and will die as one.'

Arvind reminisces the time when the BJP was founded around 1980 and his leader, the Shiv Sena *pramukh* had declared 'Hindutva is nationalism' as his stand. ' The Shiv Sena *pramukh* never believed in casteism; he used to say that there are only two castes, rich and poor. Helping the poor and needy people is the mandatory duty of every government. He used to mention that hunger knows no caste, give work to empty hands and food to empty stomachs.' In 1987, a by-election was held in the Vile Parle Assembly constituency of Maharashtra and it was the first election which was fought on the Hindutva issue. The Shiv Sena had declared Dr Ramesh Prabhu as their candidate and Balasaheb delivered vibrant speeches openly on Hindutva. Dr Prabhu won the by-election with a margin of 11,000 votes.'

In 1985, he continues, the Shiv Sena *pramukh* decided to have an alliance with the BJP based on the 'Hindutva' ideology. The Shiv Sena was active in Maharashtra and the party started working all over the country for spreading and preserving Hindutva. Although the party was established in Mumbai and Thane, the Sena soon began spreading its wings in other regions as well. In 1988, the Shiv Sena contested the elections of Sambhaji Nagar (Aurangabad) Municipal Corporation and Arvind says he still recollects working incessantly over a month in unbearable heat and suffered from nose-bleeding due to the hot weather and scorching sun rays. But nothing could stop him or his colleagues from campaigning, rather he claims they did not even notice these physical problems caused by hot weather.

'We used to feel as if a few years had been added to our lives whenever the Shiv Sena *pramukh* used to pat us on our back with compliments. The feeling was just like whatever we do, is not sufficient. We always wanted to dedicate more and more of ourselves for the growth of the party. Unfortunately, the Shiv Sena *pramukh* was deprived rights of voting and contesting any elections for six years between the period of 11 December 1999 and 10 December 2005 for using the Hindutva issue openly during the election campaign. I think he was never a victim of any inducement or temptation but believed in being selfless and spiritual,' he says.

Arvind believes his actual political journey began in 1992 when he was entrusted with the responsibility of Jalgaon District and in 1994 made in charge of North Maharashtra as *sampark pramukh* due to his dedicated work. 'During that period, Shiv Sena did not have a single MLA in this region. I travelled through every small village and soaked in the language, style, issues faced by farmers related to crops like banana, cotton. The atmosphere, weather, everything was new for me. It was a wide canvas for me. Farmers were in trouble due to the attack of some insects on wheat crop. They were neither being able to sell the wheat nor was the government coming forward to purchase it. Being zilla *sampark pramukh* of Jalgaon, along with my other office bearers, we launched an agitation in the form of a massive rally at the Collector's office. This compelled the government to purchase the 'red wheat.' The agitation proved to be a great relief to farmers and boosted their confidence in the Shiv Sainiks. Farmers started putting faith and trust in the party and this helped us grow in Jalgaon.'

Later, the election for the assembly of Maharashtra was declared in 1995. Shiv Sena and BJP made an alliance. Out of 12 assembly seats, the Shiv Sena contested 6 and BJP 6. I was happy that out of 6, in the very first election, due to the blessings of Balasaheb and under the guidance of Uddhav saheb and tireless efforts of my active colleagues from the party, we won in four constituencies and in the following elections, we captured five seats. This was followed by one more seat in Dhule and more victories in corporation elections at Jalgaon and Nashik. This was also the time when Uddhav saheb became more active in party work. He used to observe everything minutely, and rendered his valuable guidance and most importantly, saheb used to appreciate our efforts personally.'

In 1994, Shiv Sena decided to conduct its annual session at Nashik and Uddhav delegated the entire responsibility of management for this session and rally on him along with active and dedicated workers of the Mahanagar Telephone Nigam Kamgar Sangh and the *sthaniya lokadhikar samiti*. The entire team worked day and night with proper planning, execution and relentless efforts. The session was a historical one. The theme of *'Dar Ughad Baye Dar Ughad'* (goddess open the doors of power) was played during the session. 'The great Balasaheb through his oration inspired the massive and historical rally during the final open session at Martyr Anant Kanhere Maidan. His address created waves as he appealed to those present to hoist the saffron flag on the assembly,' he adds.

Balasaheb, he claims, was a keen observer and used to see everything very minutely. 'Appreciation about my dedication and devotion towards party work must have been in his mind. In 1996, he called me and made me the Member of the Legislative Council of Maharashtra (MLC). I was thrilled by this honour. Tell me is it possible in any other party? Without even requesting, thinking or demanding, my party made me the MLC. I learnt the same thing from my parents and leader—that is, to be loyal and do every possible thing for reducing the pain of sufferers. I believe it was the result of this ideology. To think that a common volunteer, an employee of a telephone exchange company like me could become an MLC was astonishing. I think this must have been a record in itself even in the history of the telecom industry. At that time, my straightforward, middle-class mentality wasn't allowing me to leave my permanent job of the MTNL. Due to this, when the Shiv Sena *pramukh* told me about this MLC position being rewarded to me, I was just speechless! I still remember the conversation between us. The Shiv Sena *pramukh* said, "What is your issue? Are you worried about a pension? Many people are standing in queue and I on my own am rewarding you and you have issues?" Arvind recollects how he called the then Chief Minister and asked him to inform the Hon'ble Governor Shri P. C. Alexander, "He (Arvind) is my son and I want him to be made MLC." I was elated. My leader, a godly figure for me, called me his son. These were the blessings of god and for me, my god was the Shiv Sena *pramukh*! And in this way, I became an MLC. My 30 years (1996–2001) of relentless work and selfless approach was thus rewarded. It's not like we were loyal because we got the positions, rather, it's the other way round—we got positions because we were loyal and dedicated. I left my job and was happy that I was able to devote my entire time to the party and with increased enthusiasm, I started working from district to district. The union work, too, went on simultaneously.'

We touched on the subject of revolts and Arvind says that he believes it was indeed painful. 'During the nineties and the following years, we got a lot of MLAs elected. When you get elevated to these positions, at times you start becoming greedy. Soon MLAs began dreaming of becoming ministers and then a few of them began living in this perception that they were bigger than the party itself. Instead, they should have been thankful to the Shiv Sena *pramukh* for he had put his trust in them. One of them even became the Chief Minister of the state. They became more and more greedy. Their egos got bigger. Some even thought of dominating the party itself. There were a select few who began to think that after the Shiv Sena *pramukh*, they would continue to dominate the party. These people first started the revolt in 1992–93. An example of this is former Shiv Sainik Chhagan Bhujbal. Where are his colleagues who left the party with him? If you look at the history of all these people who have left the Sena, today you will find them nowhere. What about all those people who went with

Chhagan Bhujbal and Narayan Rane and many more? Where are they today? How many have survived and how many remember them? Look at all those who have given both the party and the party supremo a hard time, look at their history. If Balasaheb was selfish, he could have easily made his son or nephew, who was with him that time, the Chief Minister of Maharashtra. But he did not. That is the difference between the selfless Balasaheb and other leaders! Who made these people the Chief Minister? Did they ever think whether they were capable of this? They did not even have the necessary education to become one. All they got was an opportunity. There was one worker who was made a Chief Minister despite not having a proper background. He was pulled out of a crowd, from a life of disgust he was put on a correct track. There was a future created for him. He was made an example for the others. Saheb created a space in Maharashtra, where even the most common person could be made a Chief Minister.'

On the subject of strikes, Arvind points out that if businesses survive, so will the labour. 'That is why Balasaheb always said don't go to the endpoint and shut down businesses, it will affect the labourer—he will not get his daily bread. When there was a strike of mill workers, S. A. Dange, who was the great communist leader of that era, took a rise of only one rupee from the textile management so that he could take back the strike. He did this so that workers do not stay out of jobs or remain hungry. And he kept the mills running. Unfortunately, at present, people too don't want such leadership. It is bad luck that some people are responsible for this mess. When textile mill workers approached the Hon'ble Balasaheb, he listened to the plan to go on strike. Balasaheb announced a one-day token strike and appealed to the mill workers to participate. History was created! The strike was 100 per cent successful! Balasaheb then appealed to mill workers to resume their duty as we were successful in conveying our resentment and promised them that he would follow the issue to deliver justice to mill workers.'

But the mill workers, he recalls, weren't happy with this decision and continued the strike. 'They went to Datta Samant who supported them in this. And look at what has happened. Even today, the Mumbai mill strike notice is on. Legally, it has not been withdrawn or deferred to date. Look at the consequences of it. Not only was the millworker displaced but the entire textile industry came to a standstill and the displacement of both led to the shutdown of any plans of employment or trade. The Rashtriya Mill Mazdoor Sangh, a recognized forum, could not gather the confidence among mill workers even when they had the blessings of the ruling Congress. Balasaheb took the onus to protect their jobs and deliver justice to their demand of wage hike but this was not received in the true spirit; mill workers joined hands with the wrong leadership and wrecked their own lives. The textile industry, which was the lifeline of Mumbai was devastated due to this strike.'

He believes the large exodus of Sainiks from the Sena to other parties which has been reported in the last few years is largely due to misunderstandings, greed and ego. Arvind cites that nobody has dared to call him and ask him to defect from the party. 'I believe I am the person who will always be in the debt of those who have helped and supported me. After my parents, the party is the one which has granted me recognition which can never be forgotten,' he adds continuing that patience and loyalty is a must in politics and these days everyone seems to be in haste. 'The new generation, I see although they are smart, intelligent and dynamic they are more in a hurry. They are not ready to live with the ideology. They are more interested in what they will get in return for what they offer. Politics has become a public market place—it has become a *bazaar*. It is unfortunate that people who follow the party ideology change when they come to power. Even contesting and winning elections today has become an expensive affair. There are no limits to the amount spent to win elections. It is horrible!'

He continues that a person himself can try to become a leader but there are restrictions on how far he can go. For instance, a person may have all the capabilities, but there needs to be someone to recognize him. To come in the view of the sight of people, one needs to have a mentor. 'It was because of the break given by beloved Balasaheb, we are in the limelight. A mentor is always required for that. The mentor should also be magnanimous to people. I always felt in life one should always bring forth the new generation forward. We should stand behind them because ultimately, we are not going to live forever. Sometimes, disagreement may occur with mentors, especially when the mentor may be thinking in a different way, which you and I may not be thinking. We should understand our limitations. Our mentor is always in a better position to understand the situation or have a different vision which you and I cannot have. When you feel like a mediocre, a mentor is the one who finds you intelligent. For instance, I may request something to Hon'ble Uddhav*ji* keeping in mind the responsibility of my region, but he has to look at the larger, broader canvass while accepting or denying my request, keeping in mind the entire state and the repercussions of that decision. My thinking is confined to limitations, while he has to think beyond that,' he says.

Arvind says that he is often asked whether it is difficult to report to the son instead of the father. 'Since I am used to having a different boss for 30 years how do I feel reporting to someone younger? I was fortunate to work with Hon'ble Uddhav*ji* when Balasaheb was alive. It was nothing new for me. We knew that someday, the chair would be occupied by him. He is soft-spoken and a mild person but, he is very firm about his opinions and implementations. He is much disciplined.' He says that everyone realized that his beloved Balasaheb's health wasn't keeping well during the Dussehra Rally (Dasara Melava) in the year 2011. While addressing the rally, he told those present, 'You have stood by me all these years, now, in the same way, stand with Uddhav and Aaditya.'

Shiv Sena, he says, is the only party which established the common man not only in the social, economic field but also in a political field. 'Those who didn't have any history or geography; maybe who weren't even much educated were given instruments of social thoughts, ideology, service to the people. This is true spiritualism. Making a smile appear on someone's face, providing solutions to problems is true happiness. Saheb used to say, "Prabodhankar (his father) has taught me that your wealth should be counted with the footwear on your doorsteps." Saheb gave us this ideology. He gave the slogan 'Jai Hind' and taught us patriotism; he gave the slogan 'Jai Maharashtra' and taught us Marathi pride. There are countless Shiv Sainiks who are walking on the path shown by him under the guidance of the Shiv Sena party president Uddhav saheb and with the support of Shiv Sena leader Aaditya*ji*! This is the reason why, Shiv Sena is my life, till death!' he sums up.

● ● ● ──────────── ● ● ●

Money and dedicated workers are too things that form the lifeline of any political party.

An organization flush with funds always has more chances of attracting both workers as well as winning elections. Political parties often use their party workers in various ways to generate funds to keep their party machinery running seamlessly. The most common ways of raising funds are mainly through party memberships, followed by the collection of funds for local festivals and later seeking donations from those inclined towards the party to support them in their activities. Interestingly, most party workers often resort to using non-traditional methods of raising funds under the party banner which incidentally may not be considered legal at all. In many cases there have been instances of political workers ending up as recovery agents for private clients, pocketing some percentage of collected funds for themselves and giving up the rest for party funds. All said and done, workers who managed to raise the most funds of the party, are known to automatically rise within its ranks.

3
THE POLITICAL GAME OF THE MARGINALIZED

7   Vote Bank Tokenism

India's vast and complicated caste system has irked party workers across all party lines. Many behind closed doors confess that while they would want to do away with it entirely, unfortunately, they are unable to do so. Many party workers also confessed that over the years, they have come to realize that the political parties they represent or are a part of may not necessarily walk the talk. Many pointed out that reservations have only complicated things.

G. Ratnakaran, a former party worker observes, 'Introduction of the reservation system was the biggest mistake ever made for India. While the idea may have been a noble one but the way the implementation of it has been done over the years has only made it worse. We have witnessed politics in different forms being played out post Independence, related to both caste and reservations in the country—not welfare and certainly not related to the empowerment of the backward classes.'

Ratnakar believes that the problem begins from the root—from our education system. India's educational institutions, he believes, have been used as a breeding ground for caste politics for decades. Educational institutions that were established by the British in colonial India were only to churn out well-trained clerks for their administrative offices and not to educate the masses. Unfortunately, over the last few years, these very institutions and the students who gained entry into these mainly through reservations are used by political parties to create unrest and caste tensions through protests and agitations.

Interestingly, the late Nobel Laureate Rabindranath Tagore, during one of his trips to China in 1924 when addressing an audience of eager teachers had said,

> When races come together, as they have done in the present age, it should not be merely the gathering of a crowd. There must be some bond of relation, otherwise they will knock against one another. Our education must enable every child to grasp and fulfil this purpose of the age, not to defeat it by acquiring the habit of creating divisions, and of cherishing national prejudices. There are of course natural differences in human races which should be preserved and respected and the mission of our education should be to realise our unity in spite of them, to discover truth through the wilderness of their contradictions. (Tagore, 1924).

Tagore's words resonate in our times today—post-Independence, the country which is known to be a torchbearer of tolerance and diversity towards other classes continues to witness casteism in various forms.

CASTE AND POLITICAL PARTIES

Forty-five-year-old Sampath (name changed on request) is an office bearer of the Congress party who began his political journey through student politics at Delhi University. Sampath is a Dalit and was offered a position in the party's Youth Wing when he was 20 years old. He believes that caste politics brings in a certain power to leadership, especially in winning elections, and which is why politicians do not want to do away with it completely.

'Caste protects their chair and many parties eventually in the name of secularism end up promoting caste politics,' he says adding that many political parties earlier used to scout campuses for students in the hope of turning them into party workers. 'If you are someone who belongs to the backward community, and if you are smart enough to use your Dalit card, then the sky is the limit,' he says adding that unlike students from the open category, those hailing from Dalit, Muslim or backward communities have good political careers in the long run. The youth, he says, are groomed in caste equations when they are in college itself. Protests, agitations and sloganeering are some forms of training tools used to 'empower' them in the art of caste politics.

'Earlier issue-based politics was practised through debates or even confrontations, but now with 24x7 television and social-media sites, the format of agitations have changed but the main crux of it all remains the same—sticking to the party's line of supporting or opposing subjects or incidents related to caste as and when the situation demands,' Sampath says.

Chandan Shirole, a senior political journalist and author of the book *Yodha* based on the life of Dalit leader Ramdas Athwale, believes that all political parties follow caste-based politics and that enrolling workers from backward classes is given top priority compared to other castes because leaders tend to believe that since the worker hails from a particular background, the others from his community will be easier to attract to the party. 'The party worker is regarded trustworthy mainly because he has the backing of the caste he comes from,' he says.

A veteran analyst of Dalit politics in Maharashtra, Shirole points out that presently there are 72 Dalit factions in the state each dominated by a different Dalit leader. Interestingly, all Dalit parties include the name 'Republican' in their titles. According to him, the late Dr Babasaheb Ambedkar had founded an organization to train and promote people in the RPI but before he could officially announce the party he passed away. 'Post his death some leaders founded the RPI but over the years several leaders have spilt from the main party to form their outfits with the name Republican in them in some way or the other,' he cites giving examples of leaders like Ramdas Athwale who heads the RPI (A), Jogendra Kawade who heads the outfit People's Republican Party and Rajendra

Gawai who has named his outfit RPI (Gawai). Surprisingly, Prakash Ambedkar, grandson of the late Dr Babasaheb Ambedkar, has nowhere included the name 'Republican' in his party. He is the president of the Vanchit Bahujan Aghadi (which was earlier known as the Baharipa Bahujan Mahasang—a party that boasts of a combination of Dalits, Muslims and other backward communities from the state.

Shirole further adds that unlike other national parties, party workers of Dalit parties are devoid of any training programmes; however, they are asked to tackle anything and everything related to Dalits, including protests and agitations like the one held in 2018 that brought the entire city of Mumbai to a standstill. The 200th-anniversary celebrations of the Bhima-Koregaon battle in Pune had led to the death of one man and injured several others who were visiting the venue. In opposition to this, Dalits across Maharashtra converged together blocking roads, shutting shops and local trains and disconnecting entire Mumbai for three days in a row. Merely two months post these agitations, the city yet again witnessed a protest rally of over 35,000 farmers, who hit the streets demanding loan waiver from the state government. In both the above cases, Dalits and those hailing from the backward classes came out on the roads as a final resort to get their voice heard. Though it wasn't clear what they gained out of this protest, the fact remains that the agitation surely kept the workers, attached to the parties who controlled these protests, busy and running.

Shirole points out that national parties and leaders belonging to the Maratha community and who have been dominating Maharashtra politics for decades have been instrumental in the rise and fall of Dalit leadership in the state. Shirole says, 'Upper-caste Marathas make up 36 per cent of the state's population and most political parties are dominated by them. The Maratha leadership already has power, wealth and muscle power but to keep their control over other backward communities, for many years now they have been creating leaders from these communities. They not only support their parties with funds but provide them with political patronage as well. In the end, the decision-making authority is not the Dalit leadership but the Marathas themselves.'

Shirole says that it was the Congress party which had started this trend followed by the Communist Party of India, the Shiv Sena and later the BJP. He continues that many leaders from the Dalit and backward classes, although they have their political parties, tend to be in alliance with governments. Such empowerment, he says, is merely a sign of tokenism as they do not have any actual power or authority to implement policies or reforms for their community. Every five years, Dalit leaders and their political parties are made use of for winning elections. Care is taken to see that they do not become politically stronger because in case this happens, then they are bound to defect or set up their organization. Shirole points out, 'After every five years, a few select Dalit leaders either get used to or surrender themselves to the Maratha leadership. In return, they get ministerial berths and all the perks of being in the government. They always end up contesting elections from reserved categories as they get tickets to contest only from these seats—they are never given an open-category seat to contest from.' He further adds that anyone who is born a Dalit is led to believe that the RPI is his only party till death.

As for the allocation of tickets to Dalits, Shirole observes that within the Dalits there are subcastes and tickets are allotted to candidates based on this factor. The first preference, he says is given to a candidate hailing from the Chamar community. People belonging to this caste are mainly cobblers. The second preference is given to those belonging to the Matang Samaj—they are the ones who are generally into the making of brooms and ropes. The last option is the Ambedkar Buddhists. Shirole informs that unlike other states, Maharashtra alone has a large number of Ambedkar Buddhists but the majority of voters prefer voting for candidates other than the Ambedkar Buddhists as they tend to believe that the former represent Hindus. Voters, he says, are ignorant and not updated on the caste factor and are hence unable to distinguish between Hindus and Buddhists; this is why in the last 50 years whether it is assembly, parliamentary or local bodies, the representation of Ambedkar Buddhists or Buddhist Dalits has become negligible. Also, there is no unity amongst Dalits as it is often noticed that during elections, the majority of Dalit leaders keep changing parties thereby causing spilt in the Dalit vote banks.

CASTESIM AND THE HINDI HEARTLAND

Caste equations practised in the Hindi heartlands of Uttar Pradesh, Bihar and Madhya Pradesh are legendary in their own way. Caste politics is so ingrained within the psyche of an average party worker from these states that when they migrate to other states in search of employment, they carry their castes too on their sleeves.

The North Indian factor is one such caste spillover of this Hindi heartland that has been occupying a prominent space not only in the states of Uttar Pradesh, Bihar and Madhya Pradesh but in Maharashtra politics as well. So much so that national parties like the BJP in Maharashtra went a step ahead to set up its own Bihar Cell. Chakradhar Jha, BJP worker and founder of the Cell, points out that the reason for creating the cell was the larger politics between Uttar Pradesh and Bihar. The BJP in Mumbai, he claims, is full of leaders mainly from Uttar Pradesh but few party workers and voters are from that state. On the other hand, in Bihar, he says, it is quite the opposite. 'The BJP in Bihar has many party workers and voters but few leaders. The reason Mumbai has so many leaders from Uttar Pradesh is mainly that a lot of them were early migrants to the city and over the years, they established themselves in every area of work. Because they are so well established and not only have the time but also money at their disposal, they never allowed the Biharis to compete with them and always put them down. That was why I demanded a separate organization for Biharis alone and not to slot them under the same banner as other North Indians. I had placed this demand with leaders like

Gopinath Munde and Pramod Mahajan as well. Interestingly, the year BJP went on to win the Bihar elections with a majority of votes in alliance with Nitish Kumar's Janata Dal (United) and formed the government, that was when the late Pramod Mahajan (who was in charge of elections in Bihar—especially the Mithila region of North Bihar), happy with this outcome, announced the formation of a Bihar cell. Although before that decision, a Bihar cell had already been created before the beginning of the Maharashtra state elections. The Mumbai region was split into two zones—the Central and Western. While the Western region was handed over to another BJP worker, I was given the task of running the Central zone,' he says informing that here too some leaders from Uttar Pradesh managed to wiggle in to take over the Cell and categorically squeezed him out by appointing him General Secretary instead. 'I am an aggressive person and do not entertain anyone from Uttar Pradesh. I wanted the people of Maharashtra to realize that Bihar has its own identity and I wanted to create that through the Cell. Unfortunately, with such developments, I could not fulfil this dream,' he says adding that he believes that the North Indian vote bank has swelled over the years with local regional parties wooing voters through unfair means. Beating up of North Indians in Mumbai, for example, was in trend.

'I believe it is merely politics of all parties together and nothing else. It was a plot hatched at the topmost level to disconnect all Hindi voters from the BJP. Every party was playing its role in this drama. There was more noise than any real action,' he says adding that although he doesn't follow casteism, he has witnessed it numerous times.

Reservation, he believes, blocks one's growth everywhere, even more in politics and education. Reservation, he says, created a hurdle for him in getting an election ticket. In 1996, Jha's name was finalized for a corporation ticket. He was up against a North Indian Congress candidate from his constituency. The latter, he says, incidentally met a few top leaders from his party and overnight, Jha's name was struck off the list. 'That day, I realized that settlements are common between top leaderships in all parties. Everyone wants to have their piece of pie and they will do whatever it takes for it. Irrespective of which party they belong to, leaders have their agendas and at the end of the day, they are all each other's friends. The reason such settings take place is that apart from the party, these leaders also need to maintain their relations with each other,' he says pointing out that the experience left a bitter taste in his mouth. He did not contest elections after that but was keen to get a role in the organization as he knew he had good organizational skills and that his nature was more inclined towards that.

On the subject of his state, Bihar, he says, that the latter is more infamous than famous. It does not enjoy a very good reputation and there is nothing to its credit today, anywhere. Secondly, Biharis tend to not let other Biharis go ahead. And, unfortunately, every party leader knows this which is why they refrain from promoting Biharis to top positions in politics. 'For instance, an incident took place with me three years ago where a Congressman met a central BJP minister from Bihar in New Delhi and cajoled him into giving him a much better organizational role in the BJP. When I protested against this, I was completely ignored by the party hierarchy,' he says adding that he follows the principle of *sanatan dharma* and hence, believes in the concept of Hindutva and nationalism.

Jha says that he cannot go to any other party because his principles are more aligned towards Hindutva and nationalism. 'It is a misconception that all workers are dumb. In my opinion, political workers are most knowledgeable about their leaders. While in the past, workers used to follow leaders out of loyalty now they do so only for their greed and ambition,' he says.

He feels that nationalism is Hindutva alone and anyone staying on Indian soil is a Hindu.

'I may be a Brahmin, but then I am not a Hindu if I do not believe in nationalism. Being a Brahmin has not helped me to progress in the party. Being an upper caste in politics is a loss,' says Jha.

Ravi Shankar Srivastav, CEO of the Bihar Foundation, the largest body comprising Biharis agrees with Jha and says that caste, especially in Bihar, is very real. 'It is so real to the extent that it is frightening. Here, educated people, before visiting the doctor will enquire about his caste and only then visit him. When they go to visit a lawyer, here too, they will make a point to search which caste the lawyer belongs to. If educated people in Bihar think like this, god save the rest of society,' he says. These complications of caste in Bihar are responsible for the current complex political scenario in which Laloo Prasad Yadav of the Rashtriya Janata Dal (RJD) represents certain lower classes and Muslims, the BJP represents the upper and the trading classes, and Nitish Kumar's Janata Dal (United) (JDU) represents a small number of progressive thinking people; if one party joins the other, there are chances of forming a government and that makes for alliance politics in Bihar.

Srivastav says that the idea of setting up the Bihar Foundation was first put forward by the late President Dr A. P. J. Abdul Kalam during his visit to Bihar upon the invitation of the Chief Minister, Nitish Kumar. 'Kalam has put forward three suggestions, to develop agro-based industries in Bihar; the resurrection of the Nalanda University, and garnering the energy resources and knowledge of non-resident Biharis who have done excellent outside Bihar. The task of formulating the Bihar Foundation was entrusted to IAS and former Revenue Secretary N. K. Singh.'

The Bihar Foundation is the highest powerful body in the state whose Chief Minister is its patron, and the rest of the government, including bureaucrats, are its members at various levels. Highly political and influential, it comprises a total of 21 chapters—11 chapters in India and 10 abroad. The idea of the Foundation was that non-resident Biharis across every field should come together and use their knowledge, expertise, and funds to uplift the state of Bihar and those of Biharis living in the country. The body includes members from across the caste and religion spectrum. What only matters here is that he/she should be a Bihari.

'When regional parties from Maharashtra like the Shiv Sena mistreated Biharis, Bihar sub-nationalism was evoked. Biharis living outside their state were emotional towards this behaviour and that proved to be a boon and a turning point for North Indian politics in the country,' say sources who point out that the Foundation has also worked as a nursery for many struggling politicians who have used it as an influencer for furthering their political careers. While Bihar has merely 14 per cent Muslim vote bank, the Foundation has a representation of over 30 per cent of Muslims (surpassing their percentage in Bihar), who play a crucial factor in winning an electorate for any politician. 'Every month the Foundation is visited by Muslim politicians and MLAs. The Foundation is 100 per cent political and as a result, is often used for appeasement politics or as a fertile ground to counter Muslims,' says the source on conditions of anonymity. The same source adds that MP, Giriraj Singh had begun his initial career by hosting a meeting of 4,000 Biharis in Surat. That event which was well marketed propelled him into national politics. In 2013, the BJP and JDU fought so much with each other for obtaining control of the Bihar Foundation that the latter has not set up a Delhi Chapter in the national capital.

MUSLIMS AND INDIAN POLITICS

The lush green campus of the Tata Institute of Social Services (TISS) plays a perfect background for my meeting with Zubair Azmi, Director of Urdu Markaz—an organization created by Zubair himself to preserve the once-rich culture of Bhendi Bazaar (Mumbai's oldest market) and the Urdu language in particular. He claims that India's major political developments and movements had kick-started from Bhendi Bazaar, a market place in South Mumbai. He continues that it was the central point of major political activity during the pre- and postcolonial eras. 'Then known as Bombay, this was the place where the Quit India movement was gradually built up. Bombay was the barometer of global India and even Mahatma Gandhi made frequent trips here, though he preferred to stay at Mani Bhavan,' he said adding that in those days it did not matter whether you were a Hindu or a Muslim. 'The only agenda at that time was freedom from British rule. I grew up in Bhendi Bazaar. The periphery was not just restricted to BMC limits, it began from the Crawford market, covered Masjid Bunder, Pydhonie, Dongri, Nagpada, Byculla, Saat Rasta, and Madanpura. The entire area at that time was knitted through one culture although the language spoken at that time was Urdu.' According to Azmi, the 1857 mutiny against the British and the drought in Bengal had people from the other parts of the country coming into Bombay in large numbers; the Gujaratis, Bohras, Khojas, Surti Bohras, people from Azamgarh and Benaras, and even Calcutta—all had migrated to Mumbai. There were also people from Nagpur, Malegaon and Nashik. The last lot, the Ansari weaver community too came and settled down in Madanpura and Dongri. The Gujarati- and Konkani-speaking people combined with people from Uttar Pradesh, and of course the Muslims, all gave an essence to Bhendi Bazaar.

Azmi points out that most political movements, including the setting up of the Communist Party as well as the formation of the Congress party, too kick-started from Bhendi Bazaar. The Communist movement, he cites, was quite strong in the city and included many prominent people as well. 'The Progressive Writers Group which was founded in 1931 in London by Mulk Raj Anand, Zajjad Zaheer (actor Raj Babbar's father-in-law), Premchand (he was the first writer to write on socially realist issues) were on the same page as that of the Communists. In 1932, they shifted their base to Mumbai and set up their office opposite my home in Madanpura. Even today, I stay in the same place and the Communist party office still stands there. Both their offices in Madanpura and Mominpura are still there,' he says adding that since he was five-years-old, he has closely witnessed the Left-oriented movement taking place in Bhendi Bazaar.

'During elections, they used to sit together with other members of the Communist party and write slogans that could be used for canvassing. Their gang comprised Comrade Dange, Krishna Desai from Parel (who was later murdered—it was the first political murder in Mumbai), Gulabrao Ganacharya from Chinchpokli area, the literary genius Kaifi Azmi, Majrooh Sultanpuri, Ali Sardar Jafri, Sahir and the musician, Salil Chaudhary. They used to speak so well that I would be left fascinated by it all,' he says further adding that the Indian People's Theatre Association (IPTA) (which is operational even now) known as the theatre wing of the Left party too had a large number of musicians, actors and theatre personalities as its members. Majrooh Sultanpuri, Kaifi Azmi, Bharat Bhushan, Balraj Sahani, Jan Nisar Akhtar, Sahir, Narayan Surve and many more masters in their respective fields were official cardholders of the party. The building, which housed their library where they used to conduct meetings, even today stands tall at Mominpura, Byculla and is now called Awami Adara.

These creative minds were very dedicated to their ideology and craft and shared their knowledge freely. Salil Choudhury used to teach music to music lovers for free from their Madanpura office while Kaifi Azmi, who came from Azamgarh together with other artists, used to stay at the Communist party commune in Khetwadi at Girgaum. The party used to give ₹50 per month to all cardholders out of which ₹25 used to be deducted and they had to run their monthly expenses on the remaining money. The money given to them was sourced from the funds created from the contribution of Communist party workers. Every worker was supposed to give a contribution of ₹2 per person to this fund.

With the closure of cotton mills in Mumbai, followed by the 1991 Hindu-Muslim riots, and the entry of criminals (who had dominated the by-lanes of Bhendi Bazaar and the city) in politics, caste politics took on a new definition altogether. Interestingly the first 'riots' the city had witnessed between the two communities were not between the Hindus and the Muslims but between two Muslim ganglords of that time—namely the established smuggler-turned-film financer Haji Mastaan and Dawood Ibrahim (who was then still trying to find his foothold in the crime world). Interestingly, Haji Mastaan in his later years was the first to bring Dalits, Muslims, and minorities together and called his political party the Bharatiya Dalit Muslim Minority Mahasangh. With the death of Mastaan, the party soon ceased to exist.

NURTURING MUSLIM LEADERSHIP

Born in Madanpura, Azmi did his schooling from Christ Church in Byculla Azmi where he studied in English medium and not in Urdu as his father wished. 'It was a big thing in those days. I further studied commerce from Burhani college in Mazgaon and then went on to study law at K C Law college. Acquiring knowledge has always been my passion which was why I did not stop my studies. I further completed my Masters in Arts (MA) in English literature, and later an MA in religious studies followed by an MPhil in Sufism from Mumbai University,' recalls the 49-year-old who claims that his association with politics began with the Indian National Congress courtesy his father, Abdul Jabbar Seth, who was attached to the party. A loyal Congressman, Seth at one point had worked under the then Central Minister S. K. Patil who was quite powerful at that time. Patil was even nicknamed the uncrowned king of Mumbai.

'My father used to say he was a good example of a leader. If anyone went for some work to get done from S. K. Patil, he never used to entertain them directly. Instead, he used to ask them to go to their local leader first and then approach him through them. He used to give importance and empower his worker. This was how he created the organization at the ground level and under his rule, political workers were good and they flourished,' reminisces Azmi.

Azmi joined the Congress party in 1987 through its youth wing as he was keen to serve the community and the nation. Murli Deora was the president of the Mumbai unit of the party at that time and Deora's technique of running the party was quite different from that of Patil. 'Deora, coming from a Marwari background, introduced corporate and business houses into the Congress and soon funds started flowing into the party under the guise of sponsorships for party events, etc. The party began taking money from corporate and business houses and the trend has been continuing even till today. Murli Deora wanted young educated Muslims to join the Congress. He was very dynamic. Soon there were a large number of Muslims inducted into the party,' says Azmi adding that Mumbai, and especially Bhendi Bazaar proved to be the central point of all kinds of politics.

Azmi believes that the Congress never allowed the Muslim leadership to grow and he experienced this way back in 1989 during his tenure as General Secretary of the Minority Department of the South-Central Mumbai district. When Rajiv Gandhi was the Prime Minister, the Congress went ahead and established the foundation stone (Sheela Niyas) of the Muslim graveyard near the Babri Masjid in Ayodhya. Although Azmi was in Mumbai, he had protested against this stating that it was a disputed place and would make a lot of Muslims angry. 'My protest angered a lot of other workers who were upset with my stand and asked me whether I was interested to contest elections or not since my outburst was creating a negative image of the party in the public eye. I was not saying anything wrong! It was the truth. Even if there was a temple in place of that mosque, I would have said the same thing! I protested against this move through letters and by taking a meeting of all eight Congress *taluka* presidents asking them to vote against this. Instead, all of them voted against me and only one voted in my favour. I was told by people around me that since my father was one of the founders of the Congress I should not go against the decisions of the Congress or I will be blacklisted from the party forever. I was not saying anything communal. At that time, the president of the Minority Cell was Javed Khan. He too did not support me,' he says clarifying that he had warned the stalwarts in the party that the Congress party will never find a place in the hearts of the Muslims if they did not retract what had been done. But no one listened to him and uncomfortable with this behaviour, he soon distanced himself from the party.

He claims that this incident proved to him that there was no secularism in Congress. Neither is there an open culture that everyone keeps talking about. Then, 1992 happened and Babri Masjid was demolished! 'The demolishment of the mosque opened our eyes to a lot of things. I resigned from the Congress party by submitting a resignation letter. The reason I wrote in my letter was that on 7 December 1992 due to non-handling and non-saving of the Babri Masjid I am resigning. All Muslim officer bearers of the Congress party sat on a *dharna* against Prime Minister Narsimha Rao outside the Bombay Regional Congress Committee (BRCC) office. Fortunately, there were no riots in Bhendi Bazaar but in Tulsiwadi, Tardeo,' he says.

After that incident, Azmi claims that for seven years he was not in touch with the Congress. His only advice to the Congress leaders was 'You remake the Babri Masjid and I will rejoin the party'. He believes everything depends on one's faith and perception and the deep polarization the country is facing today is due to this move. Ayodhya is now a metaphor and a symbol of a divide in India. He went on to join the (SP) in 1995 and was appointed District President. 'The reason I joined SP was because of Mulayam Singh. I thought, "Here is a Hindu man who claims he is secularly running a party dominated by Muslims, so let's give it a try." I was with the party from 1995 to 2005, for almost a decade. During that time, I spent my own money. The party told me to contest elections but I declined,' he confesses pointing out that the Muslim vote in Mumbai is very crucial for winning elections.

He feels that although politicians talk of empowering Muslims in their election speeches, once they are in power, they forget about them. The empowerment of Muslims, he says, can happen only through services or politics. Power is necessary, but leaders today are now corrupt. For them, everything is about money. Now, you need money to contest elections. First, political parties used to sponsor candidates during elections, now it is vice versa. All political parties want money, he trails off.

Congress spokesperson, Nizamuddin Rayeen feels that in the last 10 years various trends have changed the way caste has been viewed in politics. 'Earlier elections were contested based on caste but now they are contested based on religion,' he says adding that all political parties, including secular one, practise caste politics. 'They may announce in their manifesto that they are secular but when it comes to ticket distribution, then caste equation plays a major role,' he says. According to him, Muslims have never been empowered. 'If I am a Muslim I am sent to promote my party's ideology or programmes only in Muslim pockets. Incidentally, in the last elections, many secular parties did not ask Muslims to campaign for them either; the campaigning was mainly done by Hindus leaders and party workers,' he informs.

In October 2018, senior Congress leader, Ghulam Nabi Azad, while addressing the alumni at Aligarh Muslim University in Lucknow had mentioned that Hindu candidates from the party had stopped asking him to campaign for them. Rayeen, (who hails from Pratapgarh in Uttar Pradesh and was in charge of the party's Minority Wing) points out that post the 1992 Babri Masjid riots, many Muslims distanced themselves from the Congress party and joined local secular parties instead. In Uttar Pradesh, Muslims joined the SP and BSP, while in West Bengal they went with Mamata Banerjee's Trinamool Congress party. 'The Congress has not created any Muslim leadership in the last 20 years and that has led to a vacuum in acquiring Muslim party workers to even work for the party,' he analyses.

Meanwhile, Nadeem Nusrath, former National Secretary, Indian Youth Congress and ex-Chairman, Mumbai University Students Union, says that every political party has a coterie and they select the number of leaders who decide what role they should play. 'The problem with the Congress was that both Pandit Jawaharlal Nehru and Indira Gandhi and to a certain extent, Rajiv Gandhi too had a wise, astute and far-sighted Muslim and Dalit leadership. The leadership then consisted of Maulana Abdul Kalam Azad, barrister A. R. Antulay and to a certain extent Arif Mohammed Khan and even a Salman Khurshid. In Dalit leadership, there was Jagjivan Ram (who Indira Gandhi brought into the party) and then, of course, Mahavir Prasad. During and after Rajiv Gandhi, this kind of leadership was completely absent because symbolic Muslim and Dalit leadership was given preference. In this instance, there was a Ghulam Nabi Azad or an Ahmed Patel or a Meira Kumar or a Mukul Wasnik.' He thinks that these leaders never could set the agenda for the Muslim or Dalit electorate because they were never called upon to do so. 'During and in the post-Rajiv Gandhi era, the Congress benefitted from two assassinations and fracture oppositions and the unacceptability of the BJP. So the Muslim and the Dalit electorate automatically voted for the Congress. This was the key period; that is, between 2004 and 2014 the Congress leadership should have had the foresight to see the growth and acceptability of Right-wing politics in the country on the one hand and the moving of Muslim and Dalit electorate to the regional and Muslim-Dalit-centric parties on the other. Hence the growth of SP, BSP and now Chandrashekhar Azad,' he says. Nusrath observes that the party has also been unable to tackle various caste-based developments including the recent tussle for reservations for the Marathas in Maharashtra. 'The Marathas are an empowered community. Maharashtra has had 10 chief ministers from this community. Why do you need reservations for a community that has already given 10 chief ministers who ruled the state?' he asks.

Meanwhile, Madhav Bhandari, Vice President for the BJP in Maharashtra, believes that political parties cannot only function on the caste factor. 'Political parties that only propagate caste-based politics have no chance of survival. Look at BSP, or SP or the All India Majlis-e-Ittehadul Muslimeen (AIMIM) or Vanchit Bahujan Aghadi. Are they strong political parties?' He points out that the idea of caste-based politics in India is something that has been created by the English media. The politics of votes, he says, is complex and works at many levels. Many cross-currents work simultaneously in different directions. Sometimes they support each other and at times they oppose each other. Vote-bank politics, he says, is a myth. He cites an example of BJP worker, Dilip Kamble who belonged to the Scheduled Caste (SC) and contested from Pune's Cantonment area which was a reserved seat. 'In that particular constituency his caste does not have more than 5 to 7 per cent of the total votes. So does Hansraj Ahir (a candidate from the BJP) who had won the Chandrapur parliamentary seat several times in a row. The number of voters from his caste's population in that constituency is miniscule, not even 1 per cent of the total votes of the area," he sums up.

●●● ――――――――――― ●●●

The fact that the Indian electorate is deeply influenced by the caste factor in its political space cannot be denied. Caste and its many equations and permutations play an important role in Indian politics. Many political parties have thrived and continue to grow based on these equations and permutations alone. The existence of minority politics, which so far was restricted to the Indian ballot has slowly but dangerously entered into our daily lives and this many of us cannot deny. For example, the much-talked-about reservation quota in our schools, colleges and government jobs is a classic example of the above. Even when it comes to choosing life partners in the 'arranged marriages market', a glance at any matrimonial column or website confirms the fact that the 'caste factor' is very much there and here to stay.

8 Women in Politics: Dodging Patriarchy

On 31 October 2003 (the same day that also saw the assassination of India's first woman Prime Minister, Indira Gandhi), Varsha Kale, a women's rights activist from Maharashtra launched the Womanist Party of India (WPI) amongst much fanfare. The WPI was solely aimed as a platform for women getting into politics in the general elections which were scheduled to be held that year.

Five years later, the party was still trying to find a foothold and became non-existent in the following months. Kale had moved on to campaign for the rights of Mumbai's bar dancers (the Maharashtra state government had placed a ban on dance bars leaving thousands of those working as bar girls without jobs), the WPI soon ceased to exist as other women members too trickled out. Constant infighting and non-agreement on many issues were said to be the reasons for the decline of the first only women's political party in India.

Interestingly, over the years, several women have attempted to set up their political parties or fronts as an easy method to gain access into Indian politics, but in vain. Ironically, even women's wings of national political parties do not have much to offer to women who are serious about pursuing a political career. Most women's wings, like any other frontal wings, end up merely as a sign of tokenism. Many party women complain that despite being in these wings for decades, they fail to get tickets to contest the elections.

Despite 33 per cent reservation for women, the percentage of women in leadership positions in Indian politics continues to be abysmally low. Though reams and reams of newsprint have been written on the subject, the reality is that it takes a lot for a woman to navigate the harsh political waters. According to the Inter-Parliamentary Union, in 2014, women made up only 11.8 per cent of the Lok Sabha and 11.4 per cent of the Rajya Sabha. Interestingly, in the recently concluded national elections (2019) the figure for women in the Lok Sabha now stands at 14 per cent—only 2.2 per cent more than in 2014!

A decade ago, during a study undertaken to understand the role of women workers in the women's wings of political parties, I was confronted with women complaining that not much is being done to encourage their participation in politics. The findings of the study—an interview of over 500 women from different political parties in Mumbai published in the form of a paper 'Evolving Role of Women in Political Parties—A Perspective'—had women politicians complaining that even within political parties, they (women) are rarely found in leadership positions.

So, are mere electoral reforms the only way for women empowerment?

From 2007 to 2009, an exercise-cum-study on women empowerment was conducted in 2011 under the aegis of the Development of Corporate Citizenship, a wing of the S P Jain Institute of Management & Research, Mumbai (Sen) wherein workshops and sessions were held with the women's wings of three political parties of Maharashtra—the Indian National Congress (INC), The (NCP) and the BJP. The study brought forth startling revelations. Women were more interested in full-time electoral politics and a majority of them preferred to work at organizational levels of the party structure, provided they had the right infrastructure and resources to back them. The objective of the workshops was not only to impart strategies to strengthen women's capacity and promote their participation in various aspects of political life leading to greater gender equality in key decision-making processes and positions but also making an attempt to understand the drawbacks they faced and analyse and come up with concrete solutions to their problems. The study was also aimed at providing a platform for women and creating awareness, need, and confidence through knowledge and skill-building; it was designed to provide a broad outline on basic issues covering gender rights, finance, team building, social problems and solutions. One of the areas that made a strong social impact, was building capacity among grassroots women workers in the political system for effective functioning.

Around 500 women participated in the workshops held over three years while two independent workshops of around 100 participants each were conducted for women grassroots workers, who though not attached to any political party, owed allegiance to male political leaders from their local community and were keen on contesting elections. Modules like finance and gender budgeting, communications and people-management skills and understanding social issues were part of the study to learn the understanding and grasping skills of these participants.

The introduction of street theatre was used for the first time in two workshops which not only proved to be very popular but also ended up as 'tonic' to empower the participants emotionally and spiritually towards their objective of having a clear idea of their political role in society. Most of the participants were aged between 20 and 50 years with around 70 per cent of the participants mainly being homemakers. The remaining participants were a mix of teachers and class IV government employees and many who mainly worked in the unorganized sector—maids, helpers, etc. A large number of women, who made up the grassroots of these political wings, were educated only up to the tenth grade and hailed from lower-middle-class backgrounds. Communication was one of the key modules exercised in these workshops and most women disclosed that they had never attempted to speak either on a public platform or with other co-workers in any of the joint meetings conducted with their leaders. A majority of the women claimed that they had performed the role of 'audience' diligently by attending most public rallies of their male political leaders without fail. Their roles would be generally restricted to shouting slogans for their male leaders or gathering a crowd of followers (especially women) in large numbers to showcase the strength of their respective leaders on a public platform.

When a module on Communication and People Management was conducted by Anjali Gokarn, a consultant of the TISS, to help make the participants more aware of themselves and what they needed, many women used the opportunity through short exercises to explain how they often felt intimidated by their male counterparts during party meetings. Many disclosed that women were often kept out during key decision-making meetings. They also individually confessed that they did feel nervous while surrounded by men whenever discussing any concrete social issue and refrained from arguing back for two reasons—lack of political geographic knowledge and the inability to handle large and unruly crowds which most men are at ease with. Most women also agreed on the point that despite having illustrious men and women leaders in their parties, they felt left out merely because of their lack of making their leaders understand their point of view. Vast class differences exist between a leader and the woman grassroots worker to begin with, which leaves the latter at the lowest rung of the political ladder for the rest of her life.

A unique exercise through street theatre by the noted group of Manjul Bharadwaj (of Experimental Theatre Foundation) was implemented wherein the participants were given 10 minutes to speak in front of an audience in the form of a skit on why they are with a political party and what do they want for the party in the long run. Many women, it came to light, were poor public speakers or had no inkling of the policies already in place for them by the earlier governments. Most women, who had been attached to their political parties for as long as two decades, confessed that they had never uttered a single word in front of their leaders. Many also confessed that even though they had campaigned for their male leaders during elections, most of them preferred to maintain a distance because of the gender gap as well as for fear of character assassination. Contesting elections were top priority for most, but not a necessity as long as their efforts were recognized by the party leaders which in reality did not happen in most cases.

A lecture on finance management and gender budgeting by Vibhuti Patel (Director, Postgraduate Studies, SNDT Women's University) too proved to be an eye-opener. Most women's wings (except highprofile independent women candidates) claimed that they functioned with almost no financial help from their parent political party leaving them at the mercy of their male candidates or family money for the generation of funds to spend. Interestingly, few women, though had gone ahead to independently form their registered trusts or non-governmental organizations, or self-help groups (SHGs) to generate funds, had used them in their capacity as political activists to get into the good books of their leaders by either spending lavishly on banners or organizing done-to-death 'safe' public events like notebook donations, blood-donation and eye-check-up camps—not any out-of-the-box activity which could trigger off women empowerment or women participation on a large scale. That most parties have no set structure in place to positively exploit the successful fundraising and marketing skills of these women came to light. The fact that most women do manage to create funds through transparent measures remains blatantly ignored by the party stalwarts, thereby creating disillusionment amongst the educated and independent women. Failing to find encouragement for their efforts, they forfeit their political dreams by looking out for better options in other fields, thereby creating a vacuum for good, sound and honest women political leaders. The cycle continues.

HICCUPS AND OBSTACLES

Many women in the study had pointed out that women continued to be fielded from 'losing constituencies', unlike their male counterparts who were given prestigious constituencies. A large number of women did believe that entry or access to political life also mainly depended on several factors, the key one being that a family already in or with access to politics makes the path much smoother in the long run.

Too often, women gaining access to political life has often been blamed on male uniformity—that women access political life only with due support and positive contacts of the family, particularly that of the husband, father, or brother. This holds true to such an extent that women tend to be reduced to mere 'decorative pieces' and 'silent spectators'—whether in the Indian parliament or municipal corporations. While many women between the ages of 24 and 28 did show interest in joining mainstream politics, they often gave up their wish post-marriage due to family responsibilities or due to disillusionment after scrutinizing the party inside out. The prime age at which independent women were drawn to political participation was between 32 and 40 years, in both cases though, not voluntarily, but at the insistence of family or a friend and only after having given considerable time to the upbringing of their family.

Women from the upper-middle class in urban cities generally preferred to stay away from politics as they claimed that they had better career opportunities and more lucrative options outside of politics to choose from. The endless wait for that big break to enter politics was therefore not their choice. Dynastic dominance too was a major factor for independent women not desiring a political career. Many national parties like the Congress and the BJP were controlled by strong dynastic families, and breaking into their circle of confidantes would take years for a new entrant, admitted many women.

Many admitted that for women with almost no political connections to make a mark on their merit within the party structure or outside it, took up a considerable amount of time and energy. They also said that they were forced to toe the party line as independent ideas were often rejected for safer options. Communicating with the opposite sex was also one area that many women thought they were not well equipped to deal with. Many women also individually confided that they felt nervous while surrounded by men especially in discussing any concrete social issues, and refrained from arguing for two reasons—lack of political geographic knowledge, and the inability to handle large and unruly crowds which most men are at ease with. Most women also agreed on the point that despite having illustrious men and women leaders in their parties they felt left out merely because of their inability to make their higher-ups understand their point of view. The vast class differences existing between a leader and his/her grassroots worker leaves the latter at the lowest rung of the political ladder for the rest of her life. Most women had, in fact, no idea of what their role and contribution in society, in general, should be simply because none of the political parties or the male and women political leaders conducted meetings or interacted with them to generate any favourable ideas for women empowerment.

Similarly, yet another study of elected women representatives published by the Ministry of Panchayati Raj (2008) although confirms that women's reservations did help facilitate the entry of women into politics (83%). It did not help much in continuing for the second or third terms, as the proportion that got elected was 45 per cent and 58 per cent respectively. The role of reservation was also evident from the fact that it emerged as an important motivator (43%) for contesting the first election as much as withdrawal was an important reason for not contesting the election among former women representatives (39%). Ex-women representatives who faced defeat in their attempts to continue with their careers accepted that there was less social interaction and /or no proper campaigning (52%) on their part. The study also highlighted the fact that 91 per cent of women did not contest any intermediate / zilla parishad election and that higher levels of political aspiration were generally not present among the gram panchayat-level panchayati raj functionaries.

A case study, *Women in Parliament: Beyond Numbers* (1998) confirms that the constraints of family life continue to be real concerns even for privileged women interested in a political career. The lack of resources for working women coupled with their class situation and economic struggle added to the responsibility of bringing up a young family are the core issues that no form of reservation can tackle.

HOW PARTIES CATER TO WOMEN IN POLITICS

That various political parties cater differently to the mindset of a woman interested in a political career came to the fore. Secular parties like the Indian National Congress continued to attract women hailing from minority backgrounds and especially those who were Hindi-speaking (with roots from the Hindi heartland), while the NCP appeared more to focus on women belonging to the Maratha-dominated communities. Fiza (name changed on request), a Muslim woman in her late 40s who resides in the slums of Malwani in the Malad area in suburban Mumbai has been a Congress party worker for a decade. Fiza adds that the reason she joined the Congress was that this was the only secular party she had known of. However, she confesses that in the last many years, she has not received any monetary help from any Muslim leader attached to the party for the 'social work' she does in the slums to help promote the party. 'I generally collect small loans from my husband who works as an autorickshaw driver or neighbours to pay for the admissions of poor girls who drop out of the municipal schools in my area. The party does not help me in this regard, though I often end up campaigning for the local Congress MLAs and corporators by gathering women for their rallies. The only reimbursements we get is a continuous supply of food and water on those days and money during elections.'

Political observers point out that women who are devoid of any dynastic political connections were likely to continue for a short period of time. However, thanks to social media, the numbers are now on the rise and many women are looking at joining politics as a full-time career option. Dynastic dominance too remains a major factor for independent women not desiring a political career. The Congress and the BJP are controlled by strong dynastic families and breaking into their circle of confidantes, who admitted many women takes years for any newcomer. Most national and regional parties are dominated by dynasties and so are its set of loyal followers who are leaders in their own right and have created their own second and third generation of daughters and sons to carry on their legacy. The NCP created by Sharad Pawar was the first to announce a 50 per cent reservation for women when it was first founded in 1991. He brought in his daughter Supriya Sule via the Rajya Sabha and then handed her his traditional constituency, Baramati to contest for in the Lok Sabha elections in 2009.

A former President of the Women's Wing of a National Party on conditions of anonymity says how difficult it is for women to make a mark in political parties without any support. She says that most women who are attached to their party mainly come from lower-class backgrounds and lived in slums and tenements compared to the middle and upper-middle class who are a bit well off. Most of them live in utter poverty or are victims of domestic violence or social abuse at the hands of slum lords. 'A woman with no educational background and young children at her mercy often ends up looking for different avenues to protect herself. In slums, this figure is very high. The reason most women from slums join political parties is because they seek refuge in showing off their political affiliations to escape threats from both a violent husband and a violent society that they live in.'

Certain parties attract certain women. For instance, the BJP, attracts women from well-educated and economic backgrounds.

The lifespan of a woman in the BJP continues well beyond a decade merely because the BJP invests considerable time and energy in grooming their workers through social workshops and public-speaking discourses on religion and public affairs. A woman BJP worker appears more skilled and confident than her counterparts in other parties.

For women with almost no political connections, to make a mark on her merit within the party structure or outside it takes up a considerable amount of time and energy. Many women admitted that they were forced to toe the line as independent ideas were often ditched for safer approaches. Also with no system and infrastructure to train women desirous of a political career across political parties, most women end up being mentally or sexually exploited by their male counterparts who make promises of political empowerment. Most women admitted that their attempts at networking (read accompanying both male and female political leaders at all times as sidekicks) did little to give them a sense of where they were headed. 'Women are more like reception committees. We are called to decorate stages whenever any big leader comes down from New Delhi or asked to wait for them at the airport to show him that we are supporting him. But in all these years I must admit that I haven't done anything for women empowerment except attend private parties thrown by political leaders and wish them on their birthdays,' says a woman party worker.

While now there may be more opportunities for women from affluent families to pursue a political career, for women from fairly common backgrounds nothing seems to have changed. The internet and social media have given them a platform (where many post their opinions and work on social-media sites) to be more visible and so has television, but the fact remains that despite working hard to be in leadership positions, they continue to be disconnected from issues at the ground level. Trafficking of young girls, women being forced into prostitution, child marriage, single parenting, sexual harassment and women being underpaid are issues not many women politicians want to talk about or fight for. Their lack of knowledge about these social issues, policies, and geography of caste and religion that dominate the vast Indian political landscape is another story in itself. Devoid of power to make decisions, they end up playing second fiddle to their political masters.

Mr X (name withheld on request), a power broker in Delhi politics, on conditions of anonymity speaks of his experience as to why women can be much better politicians than men but unfortunately, they are bound by many restrictions. 'Our culture isn't like that of other countries where women are doing well in the political field. Politics is a full-time job and we have seen that it is difficult for women to come full-time in politics because first of all the entire onus of running a home falls on a woman. Even if her family is very progressive or her husband may be very cooperative, the primary responsibility, such as the responsibility of the children, etc., falls on her shoulders. The early years of a woman are mostly spent in bringing up the children (as the latter's first attachment is automatically towards the mother) and because of that, a big period of her life, which may be 10 to 15 years, gets automatically devoted to the family and which is why the woman cannot devote full time to politics during that time.' He adds that men tend to go forward in this period and then the competition rises, and it becomes very difficult for women to break into that competition. 'The second thing is that even today in Indian politics, no one allows women to go ahead easily. Because men feel that if women go ahead, their importance will decrease. But, I feel that even today, both are on the same pedestal, it is just that in the prime time of your life, you have to build up your career—be it business or politics; if that is gone, then it becomes difficult to again stand and take a go. Especially so in politics because after every five years there are elections, and men who contest and win tend to automatically go ahead in their careers—their foundation is already formed, unlike women who, by the time they come in, are way too behind to catch up,' he says.

Mr X informs that these days to win elections, parties decide on the 'face factor', like which face will be good for the party or win them a particular seat. 'For example, in so and so state, this face will work or in another state, some other face may work, etc. For women, it is a different issue. To date, except Rajasthan where Vasundhara Raje Scindia is prominent (that is because of her royal family background and in the way she has created her own persona), I have not come across anyone like her. So, acceptability by the people of the state, be it at the local or the national level matters a lot—then, gender doesn't matter here.' He further continues that although reservation of seats for women is there, most times this does not help the woman as the husband or the father or the brother ends up calling the shots once the woman wins the seat.

Another issue that he believes, which most women party workers face, is competition and opposition from the local-level party workers, who eventually end up forming their groups.

'And it is very difficult for ladies to break this groupism,' he observes pointing out that the most common problem which women workers face is that of character assassination. 'If she tends to get quite solid in her field, they start assassinating her character. So, she tends to fall behind. There are a lot of women who face similar things but the ones who manage to go ahead are those who not only tend to be strong and firm themselves but also who have strong family trust and support. Until women have the latter, they are not able to go ahead on their own,' he says, further adding that a few years ago the scene was such that if any woman was close to a particular leader, her name would be maligned and a scandal would be created linking him to her. And this is why, most leaders, for fear of their names being maligned or of an unnecessary scandal being built, prefer not encouraging any woman at all. 'So this fear of being targeted has political parties debating the pros and cons of promoting women. If a married woman's husband is not from politics but the private sector and his wife wants to get into politics, then he would eventually advise her not to pursue the field in fear of such *badnami*. Or, the couple should be such that both are interested and both know what the negatives and positives of the field are since only then can they support each other. If both of them know they can take care of each other through such problems, then they should give politics a shot.'

Sandhya Sinha, the founder of the Women's Political Forum, a body founded in 2005 to promote the welfare of women in politics, believes women get a raw deal in Indian politics. The 60-something Sinha, who also runs her own NGO, *Grihasti*, hails from a family of politicians and is known to be close to the Gandhi family. Sandhya also held a position in the Delhi PCC and handled Bollywood actor-turned-politician Shatrughan Sinha's election campaign in Bihar. 'I have seen the way women were treated and that used to irk me a lot. Despite all good intentions, they are treated like a ping-pong ball. Although women are more talented than men, I think they are treated very badly. For instance, if a public rally or programme is happening and a woman is sitting quietly in the front row, she is often asked to get up and go behind or stand at the back. Or, they are taunted with lines like "What are you doing in politics? Go home and take care of your family. Do you even understand anything?" adding that many times men resort to the oldest trick in the book—that of luring the women away from their objective by seducing them and unfortunately many women too end up succumbing to the advances of such men. . . . Many women are ambitious and believe that this is one way of going ahead and hence choose this path. It is sad but if such is the level that most women resort to, unfortunately, they will also experience that level of politics. For many women being in politics is for self-purpose and not for social or community reasons. Many women are driven by the ambition to have power for themselves too,' she points out adding that in such cases, women end up lowering their status. And men, she continues, want to dominate women simply because in case she becomes empowered, she will be a threat to them and they will be replaced.

Sinha's Forum is active in five states, including Bihar and Maharashtra. Originally hailing from Bihar, she divides her time between Delhi and Patna and believes that women party workers often find it difficult to get plum positions or even election tickets to contest. Thanks to her Forum, she claims to have access across all political parties and shares her observations on the way women are treated in them.

In the Congress, she says, there is neither any policy, system nor processes in place for women workers to seek promotions. 'The Congress party is all about dynasty. You may not get much importance if you are not the wife or daughter of any known politician. It is all about which family you belong to and whose wife, daughter, or daughter-in-law you are. They think that such people or those belonging to such families understand politics. The rest are not aware of it or will not understand.' Often a woman getting a position, therefore, ultimately depends on the kind of people she maintains proximity with.

The BJP, she believes, is the opposite, 'In the BJP, if you have the talent, you don't need to be close to anybody; you are given respect and acknowledgement. As for the CPI (M), there is no issue of gender at all. Their approach is that they work in every corner of the country. But they thrive to work on the agony and the poverty of the people. They are in a different league altogether.' When it comes to ticket distribution, men are given more preference because they are the money holders, they are the persuaders. 'They have money and they can sit at tea stalls and converse with the public,' she says pointing out that in many cases, politicians, regard a woman as someone who is only fit for keeping company, and at times, tend to misuse her. 'Most of the men in politics want a female companion. In most cases, ambitious women are taken advantage of under the pretext that she would be introduced to someone. They come to know that if a woman is interested and ambitious, they introduce her to several men and after that, the condition that she lands herself in, they are not concerned with at all. Unfortunately, some women get used in this bargain in the cheapest way possible. Many women are misused by not one but multiple men. She says adding that, which is why self-reliance for every woman is very important.

Sinha observes, 'Since childhood, it has been grilled into the psychology of women that they have to serve and take care of others. Never is a woman taught to take care of herself. They never teach that you are living for yourself. If you look after yourself, you become reliant and strong and nobody can use you. This temperament is never taught to women.' Even women leaders are not supportive of other women to come into politics because they think that their position will be threatened. 'It is high time this should change,' she says.

On the subject of reservations for women in political parties, BJP Maharashtra Vice President Madhav Bhandari informs that his party has as per constitution reserved 33 per cent of its seats for women in their organization, which has led to the entry of the maximum number of women officer bearers in the party.

As for election tickets, he says that there is no quota for the same but the party does consider the names of women who are recommended for tickets. These names, he says, are generally suggested from the ground level. 'Tickets for general elections like the assembly and parliamentary ones are generally allotted to those who are capable of getting votes. As it is there is a 50 per cent reservation for women at the local-level bodies that include panchayat elections as well. So we do get to see a large number of women there,' he says.

On the other hand, Advocate Rinisha V, a municipal councillor from Mallapuram, Kerala believes that being in politics is not a part-time job but a 24 x 7 affair. The 33-year-old, who is also a mother, says that she is always on her toes as people reach out to her for a variety of things—from problems of water connections and electricity to even pensions and birth and death certificates.

Rinisha contested the elections on behalf of the IUML. She claims that she was approached by the political party because of the reservation quota and soon joined the party's women's wing after she became a councillor. She says that her husband is not a party member and the reason she joined the party was not because of how strong it was but because it had done many things for the public in Kerala. She believes that politics in Kerala is different and has its pros and cons. The plus points are that they get a chance to interact with the public and do them some service but the drawback is that if they have any problem, people do not understand and in return blame them for it.

As for manipulations, she believes that women are better at handling manipulations than men but feels that it is better to have a godfather as it helps solve a lot of things. She further adds that they have the freedom in their party to ask for a ticket to contest but it is better when 'it shows that they recognize my work and are impressed with my ability.' It helps that reservation helps women to get ahead politically at local levels but she hopes that the same should be applied for assembly and parliamentary elections.

Like any other woman, Rinisha's day begins with doing the morning chores. 'My Bluetooth is on while I take my calls and my family is now used to this. They are not bothered by this at all. Once or twice, I conduct meetings at my house as well,' she says. She says that even today she works on raising her funds as she did for her election campaign. The latter cost her merely ₹50,000 on posters and creating songs, 'The party helped with the rest—manpower, funds and door-to-door campaigning as well.'

●●● ———————— ●●●

Despite a large number of women today seeking higher education and ending up with well-paying jobs, the domain of politics continues to be a treacherous one especially for those who hail from non-political backgrounds. A large part of India resides in its villages and although rapid urbanization is fast transforming these small hamlets into two- and three-tier cities, the mindset of the people residing within these places has yet to change.

While on one hand, we are creating institutions that promote education for women, sadly, on the other hand, we are yet to create a society that furthers the use of that education into public life. The idea of women pursuing careers in public life is still a nascent thought—a fact which was noticed in the recent 2019 Lok Sabha elections report by the Association for Democratic Reforms. The report states that 32 per cent of women candidates declared their educational qualifications to be between fifth and twelfth grade, 55 per cent declared having an educational qualification of graduation and above. Interestingly, 74 per cent of women who contested these elections were between the ages of 25 and 50 years while 25 per cent women candidates who contested were between the ages of 51 and 80 years.

If women need to be accepted in politics, they should make themselves heard and seen too. Interestingly, out of the many women leaders and party workers that I reached out to, only a select few agreed to be interviewed and reveal the actual happenings on what takes place behind the workings of a political party. Some well-known women politicians, despite giving appointments, cancelled at the last minute refusing to meet and share details of their long journeys unlike their male counterparts, who were not only open but also transparent in claiming their thoughts, their likes, and dislikes of their leaders and the parties they represented.

It is time that women abandon their 'gender cloak' and work towards proving themselves at par with their male colleagues on a common platform and well prove Sir Darwin's theory of 'Survival of the Fittest' correct.

4
OILING THE NUTS AND BOLTS

9 Defections and Desertions

Defections and desertions have been a common affair for decades in most political parties. The entry and exit of leaders from one party to another, especially during the time of elections, is now fairly routine. When prominent or second- and third-line leaders of political parties switch sides, it is the political worker who ends up becoming a victim of the chaos that is created. While leaders switching sides are often compensated handsomely, either with an election ticket during polls or with plum positions, or even with monetary benefits, the political worker ends up merely being a spectator in this entire drama.

Often political parties, under the guise of the membership drive, not only engineer defections but also incidentally face desertions from their party. And when this happens, life for an ordinary political worker does not remain the same. His existence, his identity, which may have been attached to that ideology of the leadership that he is following goes for a toss.

When the West Bengal unit of the BJP hosted a two-day 'Chintan Baithak' in Durgapur earlier this year, which was well attended by senior leaders and office bearers of the state, many leaders and political workers conveyed their distaste and concern over leaders from the opposition—mainly the Trinamool Congress party—joining them.

Many party loyalists believed that leaders from non-BJP parties did not fit into the culture of the party and were maligning them openly in the state. Although they were told that the entry of leaders from other parties was done mainly keeping in mind the objective of winning the state assembly polls in 2021, a number of party old-timers demanded to know why the leaders from the Trinamool Congress and the CPI (M), who had tortured and harassed BJP workers were now being allowed to join them.

While BJP leaders pointed out that the central leadership was happy with the party's performance in the Lok Sabha polls, where they had won 18 out of 42 Lok Sabha seats, their workers were not happy that leaders from other parties—without having their backgrounds or intentions checked—were being inducted into their domain.

Indian politics had witnessed the same after 2014. Post the victory of the BJP in the Lok Sabha Elections twice in a row, the party has been witnessing an influx of many leaders and political workers from the opposition. While in West Bengal, workers attached to Mamata Banerjee's Trinamool Congress shifted to the BJP, in Maharashtra too before the advent of Pitrupaksha, the Hindu period where the souls of one's dead ancestors are worshipped and put to rest—the Sharad Pawar-led NCP witnessed an exodus of its top leaders and workers and shifting of their allegiance to the BJP.

Two political workers from Maharashtra—one with the NCP and the other a former Shiv Sainik recall what it is like to be amid these desertions and what impact it creates on the common party worker.

MY PARTY, MY LIFE

For many political workers, an association with their leaders is similar to that of them being in a marital relationship. They are willing to survive both the smooth roadways and turbulences that come being within the circle of their favourite leaders.

Dinkar Hiroji Tawde, General Secretary, Maharashtra of the Nationalist Congress Party or NCP as it is known, has been following the party's founder and leader, Sharad Pawar ever since the latter broke away from the Indian National Congress (INC) to form his party, first in the late seventies and then later towards the end of the nineties.

The 57-year-old claims his life has been transformed ever since he came in close association with his leader, Sharad Pawar. 'I was born in a village called Wada in Devgad in the Konkan region where I grew up to study till Standard 5, after which my family moved to Mumbai. I completed my education in this city. It was in the year 1978 that I came in contact with Sharad Pawar saheb when he became the Chief Minister after separating himself from the Congress (I) party. I was a student then and was immediately attracted to him because of this stand that he took. The stand of walking the path alone! It was a myth in those days that the Chief Minister's position in Maharashtra would only be occupied by someone from the Congress culture and only a true and 'blue-blooded' Congressman. Pawar saheb broke this misconception when he was merely 37 years old by revolting against the High Command and forming his party called Congress (Samantar [S]).' Tawde says that none of his family members has been in politics ever. They used to live in the Jogeshwari suburb of Mumbai and at that time, only two political parties were prominent in the city—one was the Congress and the other, the Shiv Sena. But he was never attracted to any of these two parties because of their leadership.

He met Pawar in his final year of college studying Commerce and that first visit he recalls was just a casual one. 'I met him at his office where he was surrounded by his followers and well-wishers. I was introduced to him and he was courteous to me. Pawar saheb had a striking personality which immediately created an impact on me. Although I was a very small worker at that time, I made a promise to myself that I will follow the one and only Pawar saheb. He is not only the only leader for me but also who is fit for this nation. I vowed to myself that wherever Pawar saheb goes, I too will follow him and be his shadow,' he says.

Tawde soon joined the youth wing of Congress (S) and worked there till he finished his graduation. From 1980 onwards, after working in an office, he would go to the party office to do party work. Everyday post an eight-hour work shift, he says, he would make his way to the Congress (S) headquarters and spend his remaining hours there. The NCP did not pay him any salary and neither was there an honorarium of any kind. He used to pitch in for free immunization programmes, notebook distribution, etc. The money for conducting such activities would be raised from a few people and these programmes would be regularly held under the banner of Sharad Pawar's party. While working for the party, he claims he did not hold any position, neither was he part of any block, ward, etc, it was his unwavering trust and dedication for Pawar that inspired him to donate his time. 'I regarded him as the centre of everything. Not only did he have expertise and knowledge on various areas of agriculture, horticulture, fishing, etc. but he also had all the qualities and experience of connecting with grassroots workers. He is a mass leader. Many leaders make big talk, but do not even meet anyone let alone their party workers. But Pawar saheb is accessible to everyone. One can go and meet him directly. I felt a sense of belonging with him,' he confides.

So influenced was he with Pawar that he even used to raise funds on his own to survive within the party. 'During my early days as a party worker, I used to incur a cost of ₹1500 per month in organizing social activities. The fact that I had no vices helped because all that money that could have been spent on smoking or drinking was spent on political activities instead. Politics is my only vice, I used to spend part of my salary on these activities. Besides my eight hours of sleeping and eight hours of working at a full-time job, the rest of my time would be spent in doing the work of the Congress (S) and later at the NCP.'

The true test of loyalty for Tawde took place in 1985 when the Congress (S) merged itself with the parent Congress party in Aurangabad since Rajiv Gandhi had requested Pawar to come back into the Congress fold. 'Since I had promised myself that I will only work for Pawar saheb wherever he went, I felt compelled to follow him back to the parent body. When he merged his party with the Congress along with his workers, I too went with him. To celebrate this occasion, I organized a large bus for his supporters from Mumbai and drove to Aurangabad and we all, in that huge gathering, joined the Congress with much fanfare.' He says that Pawar's entry back into the Congress at that time left him disturbed and confused about his devotion to his leader.

'The reason I had decided to follow Pawar saheb was because of his independent stand and now that he was going back on his word it was a little hard to believe. Yet, I did not doubt him. Maybe he had his reasons. But, personally, my opinion would be that he should have kept himself and his identity independent. He should have stuck to his path of secularism (by taking all classes and castes together) and continued to be out on his own. I guess that did not happen and maybe that is why he must have rejoined the Congress. My thoughts on how he should have acted stopped the moment we merged ourselves with the Congress.'

Post the merger, Tawde points out, there were many conflicts that they had to face. There was no personal freedom within the Congress for the newly joined workers as well as the leaders. 'Whenever we worked with the Congress party, each time, in every region, we needed to take the permission of the "High Command". The High Command comprises a group of people at the top level. That was always bothersome. Whether it was Maharashtra or elsewhere, at that time we realized that if Pawar saheb had kept his identity separate, there was no need to go the Congress High Command every time. Because of this conflict, many party workers including leaders shifted their alliances to the Shiv Sena,' he explains.

Sharad Pawar, he continues, used to be idolized by the youth in those days—his policies, his study on a variety of issues; whether it was information and technology or even finance, he was well-read and well-informed. Pawar was sharp and even on his own could elect MLAs. His decision to merge with the Congress had affected his image badly at that time.

Tawde believes his re-entry into the Congress party was his biggest mistake, but a small party worker like him could not point out this mistake to him. He discloses that he witnessed injustice also meted out to saheb during his tenure in the Congress. Like an opportunity for Pawar to become the Prime Minister of India was lost, and that for workers like him this was a big shock and tragedy.

'The fact that a mass leader like him from Maharashtra never got an opportunity to lead the country is one big blow in life which one can never recover from. I too never received an opportunity to exercise my talents and strengths in the Congress party or rather I would say I was never given a chance to do so. I guess Pawar saheb must have felt this at some point because, in 1999, he yet again broke away from the Congress party and established the NCP. I believe he consulted other leaders like P. A. Sangma, Tariq Anwar, Praful Patel and a few prominent people from Maharashtra on this at several meetings in Delhi. In Mumbai, we too were called in for some discussions by him and told of his decision. Honestly, we were not only relieved but happy and enthusiastic that now we could finally have our "independence" as before.'

This decision of Pawar to yet again break away from the party raised eyebrows and questioned the credibility of the Maratha strongman. Incidentally, Pawar himself was known to engineer many defections and after establishing the NCP had poached second-line Congressmen to join him. 'Pawar saheb was breaking away for the second time from the Congress and I was always asked by others whether this second defection created any doubt in my mind. I was often confronted by queries from everyone I knew asking me what kind of a leader was he? He did not have a permanent stand but kept going back and forth or that he kept on breaking off from the party, not once but twice. I ignored all these taunts because I believed that it was not that Pawar saheb had rejoined the Congress only for power. The Congress should have respected him; instead, they kept him restricted only to Maharashtra. They saw him as competition, a threat, and the Congress High Command in an attempt to cut off this threat demoted him in several ways. Like for instance, they appointed Sitaram Kesari as Congress President—that position should have gone to Sharad Pawar—he deserved it. This disappointment and anger were also felt by most party workers who believed tremendously in him.'

Tawde believes that Pawar was more deserving than Kesari and the regret that he felt was also felt by every worker. This injustice was evident in the meetings that were later held amongst the party workers. 'He was someone who had kept the entire Congress clan together, was loyal and agreed to everything—I believe the decision that Pawar took in 1999 to form his party was an apt one,' he states.

Tawde points out that over the years he had been getting offers from other parties to join them. But he refused to give in because the Congress, Shiv Sena and even in the BJP he failed to find any leadership like Pawar saheb. 'After NCP was formed, I was made the general secretary of Mumbai and then gradually promoted to the general secretary of Maharashtra. For over 15 years now, I have been with the NCP. The main job of the general secretary is you have to build the organization at the lower levels across the state both in rural and urban areas including in the interiors and spread the rules and policies of the party to party workers. I believe the NCP is a party for all and refuse to accept the allegation that it is only for Marathas. This is a misconception. We always get to hear this in the media. The fact is that any leader after coming to the party, irrespective of his background has created an identity for himself in the NCP. The party gave him that space to be something, and someone. If the leader is strong in his region, obviously people elect him. In Mumbai for instance, it was

Sachin Ahir who took the lead and created the base for the party. Similarly, Nawab Mallik too created his image and identity.'

Interestingly Ahir, one of the most loyal leaders of Pawar, was amongst the first of the many NCP leaders to jump ship to the Shiv Sena. Rumours are that the Shiv Sena had promised him an MLC and a ministerial berth if the party came to power in the state elections. Post the exit of Ahir, the NCP which celebrated 20 years of its existence on 10 June this year (2020) has been reeling from the desertions of many of its top-rung leadership. But it was the exit of its MP, Udayanraje Bhonsale, a descendent of Shivaji Maharaj to the BJP that proved to be the final blow for the party.

A senior NCP functionary believes that these desertions were done keeping in mind the future political prospects of the leaders. 'They noticed that it was impossible to come to power again with the BJP being elected for the second time in a row. The vote margins were as huge as over 50,000 and it did not seem possible to cover that even if they contested on an NCP ticket. The smart thing to do was shift allegiance to the ruling party and contest from their ticket to remain in power. Of course, along with them, their supporters and political workers too shifted,' he observes.

Interestingly, the NCP whose base was founded on defections, now finds its top-rung leadership and political workers gone. Yet, Tawde defends the party and his leader by saying that the exits have not dampened the mood of workers like him. He believes the party will come out stronger from this. 'When the NCP was first formed, there were people from other castes as well—Muslims, Dalits, OBCs—but more than that, it was a party that created a pool of leaders. From 1999 to 2014, the party had around 7 to 10 politicians who were capable of being Chief Ministers in their own right and had all the qualities to lead the state. Whether it was Chhagan Bhujbal, Ajit Dada Pawar, Dilip Walse Patil, the late R. R. Patil, Sunil Tatkare, or Rajesh Tope, they all were well capable of holding high positions and some of them even did so for some time. The credit for all of this goes to Pawar saheb for creating such kind of leadership. This is yet again a phase. He has faced such crises in the past and will conquer this crisis again. . . . Look at Tamil Nadu's late Jayalalitha (politician of the AIADMK) or Mamta Banerjee (founder of Trinamool Congress in West Bengal); they have not created any second leadership. A party that does not have a second rank of leadership is hard to survive in the future, and in the NCP there is already a huge second leadership present unlike the Congress in the state which does not have any second-rank leader ready.'

Tawde believes that post-parliamentary elections of 2014 and 2019, the greedy ones within the party to further their political gains have defected to the BJP. 'In the NCP, even today, the ideology of Sharad Pawar reigns supreme. Not only do the current party workers and their leaders but even the third and fourth generation of workers are under the influence of Pawar saheb.' He adds that Pawar saheb had always helped him at every point of life. 'Whether it was to get a home in Mumbai or an election ticket for my wife to contest the municipal polls . . . there was a huge competition and tremendous fights to get tickets at that time since the Congress and NCP were into an alliance at that time. But the odds were in my favour. I believe the party recognized my dedication and trust to them. Even in 2012 during the Congress-NCP alliance, Pawar saheb gave me an election ticket to contest. In 2008, he appointed me as a member of the prestigious Maharashtra Housing and Development Association (MHADA) board for three years. Again in 2014, in the Jogeshwari assembly polls, I got a ticket to contest the elections all because of him. Coming back to Pawar saheb, he is a problem-solver to the core. If you go to him with any problem, he solves it 100 per cent. He knows every worker of the party by name and he is the main reason for my existence in the party. He is my life.'

THE AGONY OF EXIT

At first glance, 48-year-old Prakash Sakaram Raul appears to be just another common man on the road. It is not until you notice an entourage accompanying him that you get a sense of what he maybe is—a man of importance. Popularly called Babu Raul by his 'followers', Prakash invites me to chat with him about his journey in the BJP at the party office in Thane. I make my way there on a hot and sunny afternoon where I am greeted by a group of men led by Prakash himself. A former *gata pramukh* of the Shiv Sena, Prakash shifted to the BJP after a long struggle with himself and his party.

'I have always been a Sainik but had to leave the party for many reasons,' he says adding that he has always been a Shiv Sena loyalist ever since he can remember. My father, Sakharam Narayan Raul, was a prominent union leader. He used to work with the trade union leader, Datta Samant. Since my childhood, I have been observing my father and it was through him that I first began doing small work like pasting posters or putting up flags for rallies. I was maybe 15 or 16 years of age.'

Raul was in the Shiv Sena for 15 years before moving on to the Maharashtra Navanirman Sena (MNS). He claims that in the Sena, he flourished under the guidance of the late leader Anand Dighe. He used to organize welfare programmes for the community and helped Dighe by hosting notebook- distribution camps, health camps, etc., which were effective and helpful for the community and the locals. Raul admits he was in the Sena only because of his father and not because he believed in its ideology. He entered full-time politics only when his father passed away at the age of 34.

'I started working by doing odd jobs for the party and soon over the years, got to work for the *shakha pramukh* (the head of the party's area office), Anil Salunke. When Salunke resigned and contested as an independent because the party did not give him a ticket, I created my team of friends and worked hard to get the

Shiv Sena a seat. I was only 22 years old then and had studied only up to Standard 12. Post the resignation of Salunke, the party promised me that they will make me *shakha pramukh* in his place. These promises continued for over five years and still, there was no sign of the party appointing me to that position,' he laughed.

The *shakha pramukh*, he informs, is a leader of every ward. Every party has an office across the many wards of Mumbai and the *shakha pramukh* monitors that office and everything that happens under it. It is set up to solve the problem of the locals. The work is a mix of both administrative as well as political work. He claims that the party does not give money to run these *shakha*s and the workers themselves source funds from the builders, or contractors. This happens across all political parties. The *shakha*s Raul used to run in the Shiv Sena were independent. They ran without any funds from the party. 'You need a minimum ₹10,000 per month to run one *shakha*, that too if you own the place yourself. If you don't, then you end up paying to rent one at astronomical rates. In Shiv Sena, there was no issue of space, like 35 years ago. Everything was open and available. Now there are no more spaces left or available in Mumbai to build them. Party workers who shift parties have to let go of the ownership of their *shakha*. They have to build a new one in whichever party they go to. Like when I shifted to the MNS, I couldn't build a new *shakha*. Similarly, now after getting into BJP, the only way I can monitor a *shakha* is when I take some space on rent which costs me an additional ₹15–20 thousand rupees per month,' he says.

Apart from the above problems, there is also the issue of access to leaders. Raul informs that it is also not very easy to meet the top leaders of the party. 'For instance, I live in Thane and my political future depends on my relationship and personal equations with my top leader in Thane. After that, you can meet the senior leaders. In the last 15 years that I have been in the Shiv Sena, I have never met a single leader ever. Not even its founder, Shri Balasaheb. I have only seen him in rallies. I too felt like meeting him and went to Matoshree at his house. But it was not possible to meet him. To meet the leaders, it all again depends on whom you are going with. The stronger the leader accompanying you, the stronger are your chances of meeting the top leaders like Balasaheb himself. I went from Thane, but many people come from all across Maharashtra to meet him and even they are unable to do so. I do not think whether this is good or bad. It does not matter whether I think it is correct or not. There are two sides to every coin. In the end, there is a security angle to look at these leaders. If the smallest of the smallest worker went to him to complain about everything, they will not be able to listen to all which is why having big leaders in between may be important for them. But I have to say this, if every leader of the party began meeting every worker of his party at the ground level or if the leader went to every village, then any party will grow in leaps and bounds and be stronger too.'

The Sena's neglect of him led him into the arms of the MNS. 'When the MNS established a new party, they had no candidates. I was in the Shiv Sena when Hari Mali, a leader from the MNS approached me and offered me a ticket directly to contest the corporation elections. They offered me a ticket because I was strong in my area and they wanted to give a ticket to a strong candidate and had done some enquiries about me. I stood for the corporation 11 years ago in 2007 and later contested again on an MNS ticket. I did not have to pay for the ticket because it was a new party.'

He claims that when he was shifting from the Sena to MNS, the party did try to stop him but in vain. 'I was in the MNS for almost two elections. I took upon myself five police cases on behalf of the party and was in jail for 12 days. During *andolan*s and protests, when we are put in jail, even the bail money is given by us and not by the party. It costs to have these *andolan*s and it cost us bad to get out of jail by paying our own bail money. No one from the party ever sponsored our bail, ever,' he adds continuing that his main reason for dumping MNS to join BJP was the irresponsible attitude of the party towards its workers. Such sacrifices of the workers go unnoticed by senior leaders who, incidentally, he says are only interested in furthering their cause. 'In MNS, I had direct access to Raj Thackeray. He used to recognize me by my name. I was the *vibhag pramukh* of the party. It was the contribution of a lot of hard work put in by small workers such as myself to make the MNS big. But all said and done, they ignored workers like me. While we went on doing *andolan*s, the leaders of the party at the higher level used to do to '*tod-paani*' or what is called settlement with the same people whom we were protesting against. What is a settlement? Well, it's a give and take of favours. Like in Thane station, we came across a hotel that hired beggars sitting outside their street to peel the potatoes for the *batata wada*s (potato dumplings) in their kitchen. These *wada*s were then sold to the public. Since those beggars were unkempt and looked unhygienic, they could be suffering from some disease, a group of us under the MNS banner met the hotel owner demanding him to stop this. We did not mind the owner giving work to beggars—it is a good thing to empower the poor, but we protested because we found that these beggars were unclean, hadn't had a bath for days and the owner was trying to get work done for a pittance from unclean and unhygienic beggars which in itself is a crime. . . . The owner instead called the police, who in return reprimanded us and slapped fines and cases on us saying that MNS people have no work. We later came to know that some seniors in the party took money and hushed up the matter with the hotel owner. There are a lot of such issues which common workers like us bring to light but unfortunately, the senior leaders end up doing *tod-paani* and the topic gets closed forever.'

He says that even when issues related to the Maharashtra-Karnataka border subject cropped up, he and his workers used to gather men to break the Karnataka state buses. 'After some point, I was fed up with this and left. We were small workers but there were many prominent ones like Pravin Darekar, Vasant Gete and other MLAs who too left the party. I think they were disillusioned too.' Raul confesses that he preferred joining the BJP than the Congress because he got an opportunity to see the workings of the party up close.

'We had a chance to see BJP only after we joined it. Here, no leader moves around like he is someone important. Every hardworking worker is given his space. I have experienced it. They respect workers and there are many dedicated workers here. I don't think there is any corruption here. My designation in the party is that of a secretary or *madhya mandal chitnis*.'

He believes that defections at the end don't matter because all parties are the same. 'If you want to stay in politics, you should remember one thing, you need to create your own identity and importance within that party. Like I have my close set of five or six friends who come with me wherever I go. When I left Shiv Sena, they came with me. When I left MNS to be with BJP, they followed me, such is their dedication. They will come with me wherever I go. They do not hold any positions in the party as they are not interested. They are merely friends. I know I have changed three parties, but let me explain. The first time I was in a party was because of my father. The second time I was because I was called to join them and it was only in the third instance that I shifted. I had no ambition to be in politics. I stay at the local *naka*. I run a library which I use as my office. Even today, if some people have problems, issues, or in need of a hospital, even if I am not around, my friends help them out. Social work is my main thing, I have never used the party name or banner to make use for personal gains or otherwise. I don't believe in doing social work independently. Why? Well, because you get a different kind of treatment if you are an independent social worker. In government hospitals and government offices, you get a different kind of treatment if you are merely a social worker with no political connections. You are treated just like any other ordinary man. If you carry a label of a political party you do not face many problems when working for the public. In small rural areas, you can work independently, but not so in urban areas.'

Raul points out that in the MNS, he never got the authority to even question or protest against decisions taken by party leaders at the higher level which is why he left the party. 'When workers like me went to meet Raj saheb, we were shooed away from his bungalow. That was when we realized that there is no respect for us at the top level. Did you not hear Raj saheb's dialogue where he once said in a speech, "Go if you want to leave the party. I can convert one person into one lakh persons." The results are now visible. Small workers like me were eager and enthusiastic about expanding the party and taking it to new heights. We took a lot of pain both day and night to create the foundation of the MNS. The party grew too but when the workers were made to feel disconnected, then so did the leadership. The exit of workers at the ground level led the exit of a lot of elected MLAs too.'

He believes that merely making speeches or listening to leaders rant will not get one vote. 'Speeches are just to gather crowds. They are a form of entertainment or a sweet diversion for a short time. Post the speech, everyone goes home happy and everything is silent, once again. In the end, when there are elections and if there is any particular subject that the public or people find enamouring, it is at the last minute. The educated class that votes without taking any money, cannot be swayed. They cast their vote before 9 a.m. as soon as they get up. They seemed to have already made up their mind two and a half years before the elections. They know which party they will vote for,' he points out.

Respect and dignity are the two things that should be heaped upon a party worker of any party says, Raul. When a leader pats the back of any worker in appreciation he is happy and vows to work harder. Many party workers are earning well and in their way give time and energy to the party of their choice. But due to the bad behaviour of their leaders, many tend to leave after a few years. He claims he knows many such men who have left politics and are now minding their own business.

A senior political analyst on conditions of anonymity cites that a political activist never dies, he only loses interest and when he does lose interest and starts supporting a party other than his, or becomes completely detached, then it is sure death for the party with whom he has long been associated. Not only the NCP, Sena or MNS, but even national parties like the Congress are also feeling this pinch. 'This is exactly the reason why the Congress party is finding it difficult to resurrect itself in the present circumstances. The major defections that the Congress and the NCP are seeing in Maharashtra are because they are unable to motivate their party activists and party workers and are hoping that with their defections, they will be able to ride back to power with the active participation of BJP party workers.' He says that party activists and party workers give themselves at least three to four elections to see whether they can play a role in party politics of some stature. Once they realize that there is no scope despite having latent merit, they look for other pastures because they have a family to take care of. Under the circumstances, the party leadership must ensure that talented party workers are kept engaged with the party. Otherwise, in times of crisis, they may not have the talent in the party think tank at the district, city, and state levels to give necessary feedback to the national leadership on ways and means to resurrect the party. 'It is important to realize that the Congress at the national level has not been able to move beyond the known five to six known faces who actively formulate the party's policies and programmes. Greenhorns like Shashi Tharoor have more often than not been able to reconcile how national politics in India is played out and that is why from one week where he is seen as pro-Modi, the other week he is seen as anti-Modi and the third week he is seen as battling murder charges in court. This leaves the average party worker confused, and disturbed and more often than not contributes to the party worker not getting requisite support from his family to pursue his political ambition,' he sums up.

In this complex game of electoral politics, defections today are as common as changing one's clothes. The promise of ideology and dedication promised to the primary 'caregiver' is thrown out of the window by the defector when he/she is rewarded well for their services to a third party. Politicians changing parties to further their political prospects is not something new. It is the common party worker whose life undergoes drastic changes as he is required to not only adjust to one but several political masters with different ideologies. At the same time, the worker though not called upon takes it upon himself to clear his leader's name. As Dinkar Tawde explains in his story, the agony he went through to keep critics at bay showcases the fact that the actions of their leaders at times not only end up confusing the party worker but also alienates him from both their leaders as well as the party in general. As one worker when interviewing for this book commented, 'I don't think any leader today is interested in what their party worker thinks. They only live and breathe power for themselves and themselves alone.'

10 Tickets and Appointments

For many party workers, the primary reason for joining a political party is to have a sound political future. While a majority of them may deny this and claim that their attraction for being part of a political party is merely for social work, over time, the ambition to outdo those around you to reach for the perks, privileges and power that a position of an elected public representative offers, is not lost out on many.

The process of ticket distribution and appointment differs from party to party. In family-run political parties, the process of ticket distribution, as well as appointments of party workers, are entirely dependent on the latter's relationship with the family that is at the helm of the party or the people close to the family. On the other hand, cadre-based parties depend on suggestions of people at prominent positions to make the recommendations. When any party worker, despite working hard for his party, is ignored for an election ticket, he hopes to be accommodated elsewhere in government-run committees and boards (when the party comes to power). While some workers wait for that eventuality for decades hoping their loyalty would be paid someday, the ones who refuse to wait, leave their leaders and the party entirely to recreate their fortunes as well as their loyalties to another master. While some tend to be successful in their attempts, a majority of them fade into oblivion over time.

The following stories of BJP worker, Chandrashekhar Desai from Goa and former Maharashtra Navnirman Sena worker, Sharif

Deshmukh from Maharashtra are similar, yet different. While Desai, who started his career as a BJP party worker at the age of 21 and three decades later continues to wait for a BJP ticket come his way, Deshmukh, on the other hand, jumped ship from the MNS to Shiv Sena and the BJP in search of not only better prospects but dignity for himself.

THE BEGINNING

Sharif Rehman Deshmukh quit the MNS to join the Shiv Sena as the Vice President of the party's transport wing—the Vahatuk Kamgar Sena. Until 2014, he was one of the closest and most-trusted party workers of Raj Thackeray, founder of the MNS.

He meets me at his Shiv Sena *shakha* (party office in local Marathi lingo), Uddhavgad, a tall glass, and concrete structure located on Kurla's LBS Marg. Interestingly, the *shakha* stands at the very site most devastated by the 1993 Mumbai riots. A large number of Muslims living here were killed or driven out of their homes by rioters. The building resembles a corporate office. The air-conditioned *shakha* is a far cry from the traditional ones littered across the city where one could just walk in, sit down on iron chairs under the whirring fans, merely hanging out with other fellow Sainiks discussing local happenings.

I make my way to the third floor where a 20-something woman receptionist in Western attire welcomes me in English and requests me to jot down my contact details and whom I want to meet. Seated in a high-end leather chair in his plush glass cabin, the bearded Sharif greets me with a warm smile and agrees to share his story for my book.

'The second-line leaders used to insult us. The party workers were not treated with respect or dignity,' begins the 49-year-old claiming that he was responsible for setting up the MNS's first office in Dongri in South Mumbai way back in 2006. The regional party, for the first time, in an attempt to woo the Muslims, had risked stepping into Mumbai's communally sensitive area, home to underworld biggies like Dawood Ibrahim, Haji Mastan and Karim Lala. Sharif's party office was close to the same spot where Shiv Sena's lone Muslim leader Khalid Bakerywalla was shot dead for setting up a Shiv Sena *shakha* soon after the communally charged Mumbai riots in 1993.

'In the evening, after inaugurating his new office, Khalid met Shri Balasaheb Thackeray seeking his blessings for appointing him President of the Pavwallah (Bakers') Association. The next morning, he was founded murdered with bullets pumped in his chest. It was like history was repeating itself with me. I too began getting threatening calls from unknown people to never open the party shutters. I was ostracized by my close friends and my neighbourhood when I joined MNS. They used to taunt me, saying I had become a Hindu and that Raj Thackeray who was never loyal to his uncle, could never be loyal to me.'

He points out that his journey with the MNS has been not only a memorable one but also full of pain and confusion. Born to a Konkani Muslim family in Khed in the Ratnagiri district of Maharashtra, Sharif recalls his childhood days. 'I studied in Khed only till Standard 5. My mother, after the death of my father, brought us four brothers (me being the youngest) to live in a small room in Dongri in South Mumbai. I went to Sir Ellui Daui School where I studied till SSC. Due to monetary constraints, I couldn't study further and ended up working in a garage in the neighbourhood as a mechanic.' He says that he was so dedicated to his trade that an owner of a white ambassador—whose car he often used to service—impressed with his repairing skills, gifted the car to him.

'It was the eighties and owning an ambassador was a big deal then. Moreover, I loved driving and petrol too was cheap at ₹7 per litre. I customized the car into a beauty—the kind of cars that *mantris* (politicians) drove in.' Sharif's refurbished ambassador caught the eye of the owner of R A Transport, a car-rental service adjacent to the garage that he worked in. 'The owner gave me a handsome offer to ferry passengers from the Naval Dockyard in my car. I found myself driving a naval officer called S. Kumar. He used to work on a huge ship called the *Ganga* which was inaugurated by the late Prime Minister Indira Gandhi herself. Although I worked as a driver for Kumar for six months, I hold him in high esteem because he is my guru and he taught me the value and importance of time and time management. I will always be indebted to him for life,' he says adding that his contract with the rental agency soon expired and he ended up working for a smuggler called Aslam Patni who used to smuggle gold.

'I worked with Aslam for 15 years from 1985 to 2000. In those days, gold was heavily taxed and smuggling of gold to evade tax was considered to be a crime. There were two ways that gold used to be brought in to India, by air and water. Before the Mumbai riots happened, smuggling went off smoothly; it was only after the 1993 riots that things changed. Ships used to smuggle gold were misused by some people to smuggle in RDX which first touched the shores off the Konkan coast. Now all people involved in the above are behind bars. But after the 1993 Mumbai bomb blasts, there was a stop on smuggling once and for all,' Sharif reveals pointing out that he is not ashamed to admit that he too had been a smuggler and worked with Mumbai's underworld at one point.

'The crime branch has investigated me thoroughly. What I am saying is well documented in the police records.' On 11 December 1995, Sharif's boss, Aslam was murdered. 'He was killed because he did not agree to the extortion demands of the rival dons. Post his murder, I used to take care of all his property and assets, etc.,' Sharif continues. Although smuggling was completely shut, Aslam had left behind his assets in the form of a hotel, shops, etc., which he claims he ended up taking care of. He also took care of Aslam's two kids until the death of the latter's wife (who succumbed to cancer) after which he disconnected himself completely from the Patni family to start his life afresh.

He claims he rented a guest house and worked hard at running his business independently. While doing so, Sharif was introduced to local politician Bashir Patel and soon Sharif's visits to Patel's office increased. He believes these visits may have triggered in him the urge to join politics. 'Bashir Patel who was the MLA then used to stay close to the guest house. I often used to sit at his office in the evenings to chat up with him and would see a stream of people come to meet him for work or ask for his help. Observing them at such close quarters got me interested and I developed an urge to do something like this too. I began accompanying Patel wherever he went,' he says.

Sharif points out that he observed Patel very closely—from his time as a corporator to that as a Member of the Legislative Party (MLA). 'He was never with any single party. I have seen him shift alliances from the Muslim League to the SP to the (NCP). I once accompanied my friend, Tajuddin Mujawar to the *mantralaya*; he had gone to meet NCP leader R. R. Patil. Aba (as he was called) was the Rural Development Minister at that time. I met his personal secretary (I do not recall his name) and expressed my interest to do social work through some political party. The secretary instead advised me that I should join a new political party instead of enrolling in any of the present ones as a new party would help me not only to realize my dream but would also help me grow bigger in it. And since then, I have waited for a new party to come my way.'

Sharif pauses to take a sip from the water placed in a glass in front of him. His voice is full of emotion. 'I was 35 years old and newly married at that time and my wife had passed away a few months after the wedding. I was sad and disconnected from everyone and used to spend hours locked up in my room watching TV. One evening, while watching TV, I came across Raj Thackeray making his inaugural speech on the day MNS was founded. I was mesmerized by his oratory skills. He spoke so eloquently that I was floored. In his speech, he said something about creating a Maharashtra which was not only progressive but also that which would be the envy of everyone. I was hooked. At that moment, I realized that there was someone interested in working for the progress of the state. I believed that there was a party which was not interested in communal beliefs but more inclined towards progress.'

Enthused by Raj's speech, Sharif not only thought of joining the MNS but also thought this would help in bringing Hindus and Muslims together. 'I had witnessed the 1993 Mumbai riots after which the gap between the Hindu and Muslim communities had widened to such an extent that there used to be tensions between the two over the smallest of things. Muslims were suspicious of Hindus in their localities and vice-versa. The communal divide between the two had widened so much that there would be constant flare-ups over the smallest of things. People were living within their boundaries, it was important for them to reach out to each other in understanding what was in each other's minds,' he continues.

Did not Raj's stand against Muslims bother him when he was in Shiv Sena? Sharif confesses that it did not.

The party was launched on 6 March and on 19 March, Sharif, along with four of his friends—Irrfan Bhakam, Imtiaz Pathan, Afzal Bambowala and Zakir Habia officially joined the MNS.

'I approached Arvind Tawde who knew Raj Thackeray. Through him, I went and met Raj saheb twice. It was only after my third meeting with him that my political journey started.'

But alas the journey was not expected to be a smooth one. Sharif recalls how the party at first did not accept Muslims with open arms. 'For me joining the MNS was as good as trying to get acceptance as a Muslim in Indian society, we were initially sidelined within the party too. Not only in my neighbourhood in Dongri, where I used to live, but people also started shunning us especially in Muslim-dominated areas like Minara Masjid, Null Bazaar, etc. When we put up hoardings of MNS across Dongri, we would be taunted.'

The five friends bore the cost of setting up the party's logistics. 'It initially cost us ₹25,000 to create the party's paraphernalia. In the beginning, we did not take an office because not only did we not have the money, but nobody was willing to rent us space to start an office. I used to sit on the road outside the Usmania Hotel in Dongri. I set up an MNS flag outside the Hotel in Dongri and my office was outside it on the footpath, I used to sit on a stool. A shopkeeper outside one of the shops on the footpath came to beat us and objected to the MNS flag being there. Soon other Muslims came and protested. They told the owner of the Usmania Hotel that he should remove the flag or they will take over his hotel. But the owner, since he knew me well from my childhood days, refused to get drawn into the squabble and ignored them. The matter went to the police station where it was put to rest.

While his mornings were spent working at his guest house, the evenings would be spent sitting on the stool under the MNS flag. Sharif claims that they began doing small work for the people—whether it was getting the municipal water connection or helping the needy with medicines or even getting the streets cleaned up. Once, they even rescued a girl who was being forced into being a bar girl. 'We used to have a report card called Karya Awhal (Work Report) where what we used to do in the community would be regularly documented, updated, and shared with Raj saheb and the party. Once Raj saheb, doubtful of the Muslims, especially from South Mumbai, voiced his concern to me. He asked me whether people would accept his party or not. I assured him that if one does good work, why not? I believe that if one has the vision to do something worthwhile and good, you will be accepted. My team and I worked passionately for MNS and Raj saheb—whether it was agitations, protests, you name it. We were on the streets—telling people that MNS is there for you. My first agitation was against the rationing office. I put a lock on it for fleecing the public. We staged protests if we found something wrong, burnt effigies of politicians who did something wrong. Soon cases started piling upon us. There have been 18 cases registered against me that include burning effigies to breaking public property,' he says continuing that they once burnt SP leader Abu Azmi's effigy in front of his hotel, Shalimar. 'When the terrorist, Afzal Guru was hanged, I distributed sweets in Bhendi Bazaar. The police who saw me doing this told me that I had gone mad. They said my men would kill me for doing this. I only told them, "Sir, this is Mumbai, Mumbai is in Maharashtra and Maharashtra is in Hindustan. I will continue to do what I am already doing.'

Although Bhendi Bazaar is an extremely volatile area, soon, the educated and people from certain 'decent' sections living in Bhendi Bazaar and Dongri noticed my work and began to join me and the party. Our breakthrough came when we managed to break in into the corporation elections by getting 150 votes for the candidate that we first put up.'

He was soon elevated to the position of Vice President of Mumbadevi Assembly. The owner of the transport company, who had first hired him at his garage, supported Sharif at this point too. He gave him his own garage space to open his first MNS office. At the inauguration of one MNS *shakha*, Raj saheb was supposed to come but Sharif claims he told him not to come until he got him a single corporator seat.

'I was confident enough to tell him and my workers that we will work hard. Soon the tally of MNS votes from the area began to grow. It was a combination of the threes—Saheb's hard-hitting speeches, the hard work of the supporters and also the work of the party. In 2009, MNS won its first seat by electing Bala Nandgaonkar (or Bala as he was called) as MLA of Mumbadevi Constituency. Before the ticket distribution, Raj saheb asked us whether it would be okay for him to give a ticket to Bala. At that time everyone said yes, mainly because Bala was a recognized face since his days in the Shiv Sena and he was known as a hard worker too.'

Sharif believes that it is a misconception that political parties help with money. 'Until I had got an office, I was spending money from my pocket. I was spending ₹1 to ₹1.5 lakhs on an average every month. Money though came in through donations. Like if someone was happy they gave us donations or would help us out in kind by sponsoring food and water for our programmes. MNS did not give me any money at all. Not a single rupee. I did not ask, nor did they give, I don't believe they will ever give. Only candidates contesting elections are helped with money. The party does not sponsor candidates. If a corporator is interested in contesting elections, he/she needs to have the monetary backing of the respective MLA or MP of the area. Often it happens that due to cash constraints, they are forced to borrow from external sources. For election campaigning of candidates, the latter used to give money to us, not the party. Candidates used the discount system—for example, if the expenses for campaigning were ₹20,000, candidates used to give us only ₹10,000 promising us the remaining later. Most candidates defaulted on payments. During election campaigns, we used to spend on food, water, and travel to the tune of lakhs. Once, when an MLA candidate lost an election, he did not even show his face for the second time in the area. We spent over ₹3.5 lakhs of our money on his campaign. He did not even pay us our money. He is now absconding. We hope to catch him someday,' he says.

On 11 August 2012, a protest march held to condemn the Rakhine and Assam riots at Azad Maidan in Mumbai took the form of a riot when the crowd present at the protest were angered after hearing some speeches by the organizers. The riot led to the death of two people and injuries to over 50 people that included 45 policemen. The riot, according to the Mumbai Police, caused a loss of ₹2.74 crores in damages to public and private property.

When the Azad Maidan incident happened, Sharif recalls that Raj saheb was very much disturbed. 'On the second day of the incident, he called me to ask me about the entire situation in detail. I told him "Saheb, people had gone to pray but seems something else happened." Raj saheb wanted to do something about this and decided that we should take out a protest march to send across a strong message to whoever did this. Haji Arafat Shaikh, the then Vice President of MNS, MLA Bala Nandgaonkar and I had a meeting with Raj saheb where we told him that the *morcha* would look like we were protesting against a particular community, mainly the Muslims. I told Raj saheb, "Saheb, if you comment against any religion, mainly against the Muslims, then there will be a problem. The Mumbadevi Assembly has 97 per cent Muslims. I will never be able to work in my area my whole life." He listened to us in complete silence. When the MNS took out the morcha from Girgaum Chowpatty to Azad Maidan, Raj saheb did not give any speech. A day later, he called me and asked me about my feedback and how I felt about it.'

THE CHANGES WITHIN

Sharif continues that Raj Thackeray was in touch with his ground workers, but only till his party did not come to power. Once the MNS got power, things changed overnight. 'Until he did not get 13 MLAs elected, he was in touch. Until he did not get 27 corporators elected, he was in touch. In the last Lok Sabha elections, Bala Nandgaonkar lost. After that in Mumbai, the party went on the downhill,' he discloses adding that he left MNS because Raj saheb began to keep a distance from them.

'Even if we got an appointment to meet him, he would refer us to someone else to listen to our woes. We were asked to get in touch with the AC Cabinet—a group of second-line leaders who would sit the whole time in an air-conditioned office. This second line leadership did not speak properly to the workers, they never replied to our queries. A lot of MNS workers who were fans of Raj saheb, those who used to work for him with their heart and mind, were ignored or disrespected. Upset at being treated like this, they quit the party in large numbers. I realized that a common party worker had no respect and dignity within the party. Through my *shakha* President, Anil Nagare, I complained about this to him. In my complaint, I said "Saheb we are your *sewaks*. We don't have respect—*maan* and *samman*. Your *netas* have all of that." He assured me that he would look into it.'

To replace old committee members with new ones in the party, Raj saheb had created a structure wherein *vibhag pramukh*s were invited to suggest three names that they felt fit. Sharif continues that they were required to provide reasons as to why they were replacing the old ones and mention their mistakes too. The three people suggested would be interviewed and out of the three, the best fit found by the interviewers would be selected. 'Post the defeat of the MNS in the elections in Mumbai, I too was called and asked who I would like to replace from my team. The meeting had other MNS leaders like Bala Nandgaonkar, Pravin Darekar, Asha Nanvedi and Shirish Sawant. They asked me what changes I wanted to be done in my team, whether I would want to replace my ward president or anyone else. I said no but asked them to share their strategy for changes in their areas instead but they refused to do so. I did not understand this attitude. I felt stifled and suffocated. If the party talks of transparency, then that should apply to everyone. After that, I wrote a four-page resignation letter to Raj saheb. When I went to give him the letter, Raj saheb asked me what it was. I told him that it was my resignation. He asked me why I was resigning. I told him that my reasons were mentioned in the letter and that he should read it. He refused to accept it and asked me to go and continue to do my work,' he says.

Soon after that, Sharif began receiving calls from Bala Nandgaonkar and Shirish Sawant; they wanted to meet him to convince him to take back his resignation. But he refused to meet them.

'I was Raj saheb's worker and supporter and I wanted to meet only Raj saheb,' he says adding that before the elections, he had access to Raj saheb but after the elections were over, his access to him was limited.

'I could no longer meet him when I wanted to. In the letter, I had poured out my heart, I was in tears at that time. I worshipped Raj saheb and was ready to die for him. Many like me were ready to lay their lives for him. I had paid a huge price in the name of politics. Not only was I spending my monthly income on various political expenses but due to my involvement in politics, my personal life, as well as work too, had got disturbed. When campaigning for the Lok Sabha polls I did not sleep for months and instead ended up being sick and hospitalized for three days.'

'Was it my attraction for power that I joined the party? I don't know. It is not only about power but also the fact that one gets an opportunity to do something for society. I always had an urge to give something back to society, my community and I found a way through MNS to do that. MNS had a certain power, people used to be scared of the party, so work used to happen easily. The day I resigned, 1,500 people left the party with me. The set-up created by me fell the day I quit. Today, the shutters to the MNS office in Dongri are closed. The Shiv Sena flag now stands in its place,' he continues adding that when he quit, Haji Arafat Shaikh, too tried to convince him to return. But, later, he too quit the party. 'He was an old friend of Raj saheb, during his Vidyarthi Sena days, who had quit the Sena to go and join the MNS. He was one of his oldest friends. But due to the AC cabinet, he too was sidelined and never got a chance to talk to Raj saheb. Both Haji and myself got together to discuss what should we do then that we had quit the party. We had quit without planning anything in mind. We did not leave MNS due to personal attacks or racism, for money or caste issues. We left merely because we had no access to Raj saheb. When we used to take our workers to meet him, even after getting an appointment he refused to meet. Most times, we were driven out of his bungalow by his security. It was insulting. If this is the case, how can we go to the public and demand votes on his behalf?

When Haji rejoined the Shiv Sena, I too joined the party with him. I had to join some party. I realized that you cannot do social work as a common man, no one takes you seriously. If you have the party banner behind you, things get done faster. My joining the Sena has helped the Shiv Sainiks get good access to the Muslim community. Traditional vote banks are now changing. You cannot often use the power of money to spin votes in your favour every time. You need to create a better leadership. Not all Muslims want money, they want better facilities and a promise for a better life. They want to see the work done in the community for them. Raj saheb never came personally to solve the problems of the people. I was the face of the party at the ground. They came to me. The Muslims came to me. Now that I have left MNS, they will not go to Raj saheb but they will come to me.'

Sharif has now moved on from the Shiv Sena to join the BJP as President of its state's transport wing. He hopes his expertise will be utilized well this time though.

But another BJP loyalist and party worker from Goa claims it does not make any difference to him whether his party realizes his potential or not. He believes workers like him who are created out of a cadre do not follow any single entity but the ideology of the party instead. Goa, which is renowned for its sunny beaches and penchant for holidaying tourists, also hides yet another secret. One of the smallest states in the country, 42-year-old Chandrashekar Desai—a hard-core BJP loyalist from Bicholi—claims that Goa is not only the most politically savvy but its voters too are the most sensitive ones.

ELECTION TICKETS AND THE COMMON PARTY WORKER

It took over three decades for Chandrashekar to create a base for the saffron party in Goa.

'I was merely a young 21-year-old who had just graduated and was given the position of Yuva Morcha President from Sawantwadi. This was before the BJP came to power here. Since I belonged to the Maratha caste (and there was no person from that caste here), I was brought in to create awareness by an RSS party worker called Vijay Marathe. I remember he had made over 25 rounds to my house to convince me to join the party since the villagers had told him that I was the only educated one here. He wanted me to create awareness about the party and hence had even offered me the position of President of the Youth Wing then,' he recalls continuing how he was 'trained' in the ideology of the RSS through many *baithak*s and training camps.

After a year or two, Chandrashekhar was given a ticket to contest the zilla parishad elections which he lost by a mere 14 votes. 'At that time two elections were happening—the panchayat elections and the zilla parishad elections and I believe the people got confused they did not understand the symbol,' he says further adding that it cost him ₹25,000 at that time.

Now, to contest the zilla parishad elections, the candidate is required to spend at least a minimum of ₹15 lakhs to be guaranteed of a win, he informs. 'You may belong to a good background, both socially and academically, but if you don't spend money you have no chances of being elected,' he points out adding that in the end, it is the voters who pocket the money.

Distribution of money happens at the booth level. The party, he says, has a '*shakti kendra*' at every village who manages the booths. The money he says is allotted through the *kendra* as an honorarium to the booth presidents who further distribute it to the ground level below to accommodate the winning votes—which are mainly large and small families, youth federations, women SHGs, including the many football associations the state has. He informs that voters, especially in villages, demand a minimum of ₹500 per vote plus they ask them to do their work like laying of roads, pipes, etc., as well. A few years back candidates used to distribute ₹100 as a goodwill gesture to the voters asking them to go and party but now people themselves ask that what will they be given in return for their vote. Goa is the most expensive of all states to contest elections as the demand for money by voters can shoot up to ₹2,000 per head,' he says adding that candidates today need to have two things to win—the power of money and muscle power.

The muscle power, he continues, also comes at a cost. 'Workers attached to the party worker too need to be given money. The cost of maintaining one person as muscle power every year (excluding food and travel) costs anywhere between ₹1 to 2 lakhs per year. The job of that person will mainly be to hang around me, do my work, follow me everywhere, be there for my work, do *zabardasti* as and when and wherever required, etc. He will eventually be known as 'my man.' he continues pointing out that despite doing all of this one isn't guaranteed of getting an election ticket.

'To get a ticket to contest elections, one needs to follow several "protocols". You not only need to develop relations with your colleagues at the grassroots but also be in touch with the top brass within the party's hierarchy. You need to maintain relations with everyone—from the bottom to the top,' he adds. 'It all depends on how your relations are and you are close to whom at the top.'

The first 10 years of a worker's life, thus, go in learning what the party is all about and understanding the situation the party is in.

'When I initially joined the BJP, the party was regarded as untouchable in Goa. Now it has become quite big,' he says. The party never provided him with any money; he had been spending money from his pocket by dipping into funds created through his business of selling cashews.

Politics, he says, is a full-time affair and often good party workers never have the support of their family for such kind of things. 'I could have easily taken up a job but I did not. My family too never supported me. I am the youngest of two brothers and two sisters. It was only after I lost my first election by 14 votes that I realized I had to set myself up well first and hence started devoting time to my business. I had a good image, the then education minister, Dattaji Rane had come to campaign for me. He had from his pocket donated some money for my campaign as well. But then I lost. When you enter politics, no one asks you why you have come. But when you lose an election, you are immediately regarded as a failure. I realized that I would have to make myself stronger by creating more money as money is strength. I retreated a little and thought I would focus on my business. I started concentrating on setting up a house, business, my shop, and in the 15 years, I have made myself secure. Over the years, I have managed to create a nest for myself with my home, business, etc., but still my wife and kids complain about me continuing to do this political work which unfortunately does not benefit me in any way," says Chandrashekhar, who over the years continued to keep his links with the party and is now appointed the District President of the zilla cooperative sector which includes credit societies, small banks, factories, etc. His main job, he says, is to introduce BJP party workers by appointing them on committees that run these credit societies and factories.

'Party workers who cannot contest elections or don't get tickets to contest are appointed on committees of cooperative banks, factories, and in various such sectors. My main task is to help them gain entry into such areas which eventually helps the party take over the businesses. The party with the maximum number of appointees eventually controls these businesses and is involved in their decision processes as well.' He points out that for almost a decade, he was struggling not only within the party but also in his business. 'Merely being in politics was not helping me in any way at all. My first decade in politics was a total waste. It was mostly social work and social work. I had enrolled over 100 patients who were serious at the Goa Municipal Corporation hospital at one time. My mind at that time was bent towards doing social work. Everyone in Goa used to call me whenever they had a problem. Instead of the doctor, they used to call me because I not only used to take them to the hospital but also spent money on their medicines, food, in fact on everything.'

He recalls that when he had joined politics in 1998, he had approached the late Manohar Parrikar of the BJP (who was the Leader of Opposition at that point in the state assembly) to stop the demolishment of his small stall that sold cashews alongside Calangute beach. 'I remember the Congress party was in power at that time and some people from their party were pressurizing the sarpanch and the landowner there to remove my stall. I had approached Parrikar asking him to help me but all he told me was that he couldn't do so as he did not have any influence over these people. So, in the end, these political connections never helped in my work unlike people say it does,' he says.

Although he does agree that to get ahead in politics one needs a godfather, he believes that since he comes from a cadre-based background, he does not feel the need for one. Chandrashekar says that by the time he reaches his fifties, he would like to contest the assembly elections and become an MLA. For this, he is ready to wait as long as it takes. 'I don't mind waiting for this. Workers like me have a certain love for the party which is beyond everything else. I love my party. Even if the party gives me a promotion, I will work even and if it does not give me a promotion, I will work anyway. It makes no difference to me,' he clarifies continuing that workers like him are connected to the party through certain emotions.

POLITICAL MINDSETS

He shares that unfortunately, party workers joining the BJP today do not share the same views that maybe old workers like him do. 'It has become more commercial now. Even if I don't get a ticket today and someone else gets it instead of me, I will never leave the party. Since people like me are cadre-based workers, our work towards our party is with dedicated emotion. The principles that have been inculcated in us are so deep that is impossible to change now. Even if we don't like the BJP, the way it is now we will never stop working for it,' he says, further adding that unlike in other parties, leaders are very much accessible within the BJP especially in Goa. 'Unlike in other states, where ministers roam around with full Z security and bodyguards in front and behind them, you won't find any ministers in Goa doing that which is why you can easily go up to them and meet them. They are also very informal and simply dressed,' he says adding that it is easy to meet these big leaders because they do not have any airs. 'People are not that very star-struck and in Goa, there are very few defections happening."

As far as ticket distributions go, in Goa, says Chandrasekhar, the cost of contesting an assembly election is more than that of parliamentary elections. 'Compared to other states, the voters of Goa comprise only Hindus and Christians are they are quite sensitive. If you take any subject, they will immediately give their response on that,' he says adding that the cost of contesting one assembly seat can be anywhere between ₹3 and ₹4 crores.

If the number of MLAs desirous of contesting is more than in other states, the rates automatically rise. He emphasizes that the role of money, manpower, and relying on manipulations should not be ruled out and that it is very difficult for an honest party worker to become a leader.

'For a party worker to become a leader is a very difficult process. If anyone says that politics is very easy, it is not. To come in politics and then to become a leader is tough. In one way you can become a successful businessman but to become a successful politician, you cannot become one so easily. Apart from a strong financial background, the person needs to be part of an incident or circumstances that may eventually lead him to become a leader,' he informs adding that the party of late has been 'importing' leaders from other parties which eventually leads to the original party worker feeling demotivated. He believes that leaders who defect from one party to another end up not only eclipsing the party workers but also eventually sidelining them completely.

When a powerful leader comes into the BJP, he is placed above the original party worker. 'When a powerful leader comes from another party, the party worker is forced to listen to his orders because he is a powerful man at that stage. The lower party worker has to adjust to his whims and fancies. Even if I complain to my seniors about this, the latter will eventually tell me to adjust,' he trails off with a sad smile.

●●● ─────────── ●●●

For any political worker, the acknowledgement of their services through rewards like election tickets or appointment on government committees apart from helping them boost their morale also encourages them to do better for their party. By elevating them to higher positions within the party structure not only encourages them but also sends across signals to other workers that their generosity shall never remain unrewarded. Unfortunately, in politics, generosity comes with a price and a heavy one too. When common workers like Sharif Deshmukh, or Chandrashekhar Desai, driven by the ideology and drive of giving something back to society through politics are categorically sidelined or ignored by their political masters (who high on power, fail to read the signs around them), the repercussions can be fatal.

The very foundations of the parties they created stand to fail. Like Sharif, many workers have exited the Maharashtra Navnirman Sena over the years. Today, the party has only one seat to its credit in the state assembly and had to undergo a re-branding exercise with a change in its party flag and logo to attract a different set of votes. Now, only time or a different 'Sharif' will tell whether the exercise has been worth it.

# 11 Political Leaderships

Born to rule. It is a secret superior force. It doesn't spring from bothersome artifice, but from a nature born to rule.

Baltasar Gracian

Seventeenth-century Spanish writer Baltasar Gracian, also a Jesuit scholar of his time, was a keen observer of many in positions of power. In his book *Art of Wordly Wisdom*, Gracian aptly defines the art of leading and leadership through several rules, amongst them being the ability of the leader to identify within the quality of leadership and creating its own set of followers.

On the qualities a ruler needs to exhibit, Gracian in the book writes, 'Everyone succumbs to such a person without knowing why, recognizing the secret strength and vigour of innate authority. People like this have a worldly character: kings by merit, lions natural right. They seize the respect, the heart and even the minds of others. When blessed with other gifts, they are born to be political prime movers. They can accomplish more with a single feinting gesture than can others with a long harangue.' As for people with a keen sense of observation, he states, 'A person with sharp observation and sound judgment rules over objects and keeps objects from ruling him. He plumbs the greatest depths and studies the anatomies of other people's talents. No sooner does he see someone than he has understood him and judged his essence. With rare powers of observation, he deciphers even what is most hidden. He observes sternly, conceives subtly, reasons judiciously: there is nothing he cannot discover, notice, grasp, understand.'

Gracian's rules, though archaic, holds even today. Especially so in the Indian political landscape which is dotted by leaders, both big and small, old and new, trying hard to create, recreate, or simply looking to survive in the political legacies they have woven or weave for their future.

Political analysts believe that leaders hailing from dynastic political families have it much easy. 'They already have a platform available for them and easy access to people and positions as well as the power to control them,' observes one.

Today 30 per cent of MPs (*Tribune* 2019) in the present Lok Sabha come from political families. Many political families believe in keeping power within the families and hence the distribution of tickets is largely done keeping in mind their families and relatives. A study by researchers at Harvard University and the University of Mannheim shows that both the Congress and the BJP are not that different from each other—since 1999, while the Congress party had 36 dynastic MPs in the Lok Sabha, the BJP had 31!

According to *The Print* (8 March 2019), India has around 34 powerful political families spread across the states. From the Abdullahs of Jammu and Kashmir to the Hoodas of Haryana, and from the Thackerays of Maharashtra to the Yadavs of Uttar Pradesh—the list is endless.

CONFESSIONS OF A BORN DYNAST

Every week, Sayyid Munavvar Ali Shihab Thangal, President of the IUML, one of the oldest and influential political parties of Kerala interacts with hordes of visitors at his home in Kerala.

Munnavar Ali hails from the dynastic Thangal clan and every Tuesday, the 42-year-old's lavish property in Mallapuram is packed with visitors of all ages, men and women, children even, who seek out the leader for guidance and help.

'He is the incarnation of the Prophet to us. We can approach him anytime,' says the 21-year-old Faiz, a first-year student of commerce who claims to be a follower of Ali and swears allegiance to him.

The IUML was founded in 1948 and its Youth wing in the year 1971–72. Ali claims to have been in- charge of the Youth Wing for the last three years then. 'I was inspired by my father. When I was young, I used to see the work he was doing. I used to witness a lot of political party meetings, mass gatherings, etc. Very important political meetings used to be held here in this house. When he graduated, my father took over as President of IUML. He understood that it was the main important platform to serve the people,' He says that his grandfather too was the one who had been instrumental in getting empowerment education especially for women too—that created a revolution of sorts. 'These kinds of changes happened when they were in leadership and my father, although he was a political leader, he was very keen on education empowerment in our region. So, he was also leading a lot of educational institutions here which also included engineering colleges, etc.'

Munnavar Ali cites that when he was a college student, he used to help his father. During his travels with him whenever he went for meetings, he used to handle the people who would come to see him. 'Till I finished my studies, I was away, I came back in 2003. I was in Malaysia and Chennai and then I did my first degree in English Language and Literature at Farook College, University of Calicut. And later on, I went to Malaysia to do my second degree in Islamic Theology in the Human Science stream,' he recalls continuing that when he came back he had the passion to work. 'I was also a committee member of many organizations while I was studying. So, when I came back, I felt that what my father was doing was the best service to society, so I was passionate about helping him too.'

Does coming from a dynastic background make it easy for a lot of things, I ask. To which he replies, 'I was already working with these people when my father was alive so I developed good communication and rapport with them. It's not like that my position in the youth wing is not a traditional or an ancestral thing. The youth league is different. My previous president wasn't from my family. The Presidentship of the IUML was there in our family before because of the people. They have been electing us as President all these years because they have confidence in us,' he points out.

He clarifies that the position did not come to him from the family but the party.

'There was a council meeting and it was here that the members of the council decided on this position. A proposal came from the party leader. Our national secretary had announced so people just accepted that decision. I am the youngest son of my father; my brother is Sayyid Basheer Ali Shihab Thangal and also into politics and education. My father's brother is a district president and a prominent leader. My father has two children, two boys and three brothers. The first brother is the IUML Supremo President, the second one is the district president of IUML and the other one is more into religious activities. He is also the constituency President. So, all our family members are into serving the people though their designations may be different,' he adds confessing that they are not very keen on getting these positions because they have a lot of things to do, but it is the people who are compelling them to lead.

'When my father died, my uncle was the successor. He was very reluctant, but the leaders came and talked to him about the importance of this because for decades people have trusted our family. We have the influence. When we say something, people accept it. So, it becomes easy for the party to control mainly because the decision comes from the family. And people accept that. Like for instance when we declare a candidate in the elections, it is the President from our family who declares it. Due to this, there are no controversies in our party compared to other political parties.'

He further adds that his youth wing currently has more than 10 lakh members. 'We are a part of minority politics. We aimed to join in on democracy. The importance of democracy is that many people are not aware of it. We aim to unite Muslims in a democratic system so that they have access to the decision-making body that was our focus. Our leaders understood that in the democratic country, Muslims (since they were not in politics) were not aware of the importance of politics, so they tried to build a bridge between them and democracy and make them a part of that,' he explains.

Munavvar Ali says that being a leader isn't all that easy, it is a tough job managing people especially when it comes to the selection of party workers or where candidates are concerned. 'We look into all aspects, the merits and performances, their acceptance in their constituency we discuss that with all the local people.' When faced with dissent within the party, he tries to talk to them especially during election time when the distribution of tickets happens.

'Those who are not given tickets, we try to talk to them and convince them telling them that there will be another opportunity for them. We accommodate them by giving them another designation or a position in the party or we appoint them to some position in government boards either as Chairman or Director.'

Priority is given to meritorious candidates. There are many aspirants for tickets, but Munnavar Ali adds that before the names are declared, the aspirants are called and interviewed. The ones who do not get a ticket are told of the decision and convinced of getting another chance. 'We tell them that this is the situation and this is the winning strategy that we have decided for the party and we ask them to please cooperate,' he says.

'It is not a one-man show. All of the party machinery sits together and discusses with each other. It is a democratic way,' he adds pointing out that creating leaders might not be as easy as one thinks. 'There are plenty of people who are very committed and very sincere as a public worker, social worker. They are all very active on the ground but we do keep having leadership training programmes for them time and again.' These leadership trainings are conducted through residential camps across all levels of workers—for the state committee, for district committees, etc. 'We call in external experts and various modules are taught. These modules are customized for the party. We teach them about the quality of leadership that one should inculcate, ways of developing organizations, etc. Some people do not get opportunities, who never come to the parliamentary stream, who never contested elections.' Running a party can be a very expensive affair. But they have a party fund system in place allowing them to collect money from grassroots workers.

'One strategy of ours, for now, is having a membership drive wherein every member should contribute ₹150 per person. This is to raise funds for the party. In this one-month campaign, we are planning to raise ₹50 crores; so each member must raise ₹150. Apart from that we also have other liabilities like running our newspaper, etc.' The party also has the responsibility of funding the election campaigns of their candidates.

'We all take care of our candidates. We provide 60–70 per cent of funding. Recently we had byelections where the party provided funding for that as well.' Contesting elections in Kerala too has become expensive but compared to neighbouring states like Karnataka and Tamil Nadu, it is still cheap. He says that while the assembly seats may cost around ₹50 lakhs or so, the parliamentary seats incur a cost of anywhere between ₹4 to 5 crores. He also adds that the issues of the Indian Muslim differ from state to state and so does the election campaigning and strategy. 'In Kerala, we have made each and everyone aware of the importance of politics and democracy. And we also give opportunities for them to participate in various decision-making bodies such as the panchayat by providing them with opportunities. Unlike what I understand from the people of Bengal and other parts of Bihar is that Muslims there have been used as vote banks—they are mainly used to negotiate, they are not much politically aware of their importance. And that is a difference I feel, in Kerala for instance, even an autorickshaw driver himself knows each and everything about politics and things like that. So, in Kerala, everybody is aware of politics and they have their own opinion on that. But when we go to other parts of the country, many Muslims don't even know who the Chief Minister of that state is or they are not even aware of their current political situation. When I was in Mumbai for instance, I did not see any drive amongst them. Unlike in Kerala, here when we conduct elections, we feel it in ourselves and the atmosphere around us.'

He does agree that voters too over the years have got into the habit of demanding money from political parties but it is not so much rampant in Kerala. He points out that at times the opposition parties do try to bribe the voters but that culture has not yet reached Kerala.

BEING A LEADER

Hailing from one of the oldest and traditional political families of the state, the dashing and charming leader confesses that he does not take his position for granted. 'I believe it is a kind of duty that I have to do. We look at the work that our forefathers have done for the community and society and feel obliged to do it,' he confesses saying that if he had not been a politician, he would have been a diplomat.

'When I was studying in Malaysia I was very passionate about serving as an international diplomat. I had a lot of good friends from around the world with whom I still communicate. So, I had the feeling that I should go beyond that but when I came back, I got drawn into the work for the society. My father was alone at that time and so I was trying to help him as well,' he says. He did not have the freedom to do his own thing. 'Actually, our schedules are designed by others. We do not have the complete freedom to just take time off for ourselves; people around here come to us for help at all times and our presence is needed in many of their activities as well,' he says pointing to the extensive changes he had introduced in his party ever since he had taken over. He is happy that people had accepted these changes. 'We just need to convince them that the times we are presently living in is changing fast and that we are no longer dwelling in the past.'

He continues that his vision for both his party and for Muslims, in general, is vast but at times, it is restricted. 'The restriction we have is that no one from the family ever contested elections. Once you are in the Parliament only then do you have a platform to not only talk but also be more visible and get more accepted for your views. Still, we haven't broken that system that we had. Yet, there are other things that we can do and we have people from our party who are performing in Parliament. Currently, we have four MPs, one in the Rajya Sabha and three in the Lok Sabha. For instance, one of our seniormost MPs, E. T. Mohammad Bashir is now doing a lot of things across India—he is helping people build schools and madrassas. We also have P. K. Kunhalikutty who too is an MP and National Secretary of the party. We refrain from making aggressive speeches as other Muslim leaders would normally do,' he claims pointing out that making aggressive speeches is not necessary unlike Muslim leaders from other parties who resort to the same.

'I don't think it is necessary. We believe that under the Congress, many parties can join together and fight against fascism. But certain stand-alone Muslim leaders contest elections and resort to splitting the votes, especially the Congress votes.' Although the IUML has always been an alliance with the Congress Party, the party has, over the yeara, introduced separate frontal wings for their workers—especially those hailing from the backward classes.

Thanks to the reservation system in India, it has become necessary for parties today, he says, to have these wings. It also becomes easier for them to train people. Munavvar Ali believes that reservation is something that was designed to overcome backwardness and the opportunity for the community to enhance itself. 'Those from the minority classes do not get too many opportunities or chances which is why I think that if there are some rooms for a reservation it will benefit the community.' He further adds that the party has been at the forefront in giving women opportunities as well. 'The IUML has a women's wing too and we are always trying our best to accommodate women as we believe that they can do very well, in fact, far better than men. I have seen a lot of girls and women who are more active and do result-oriented work. I think if we give them opportunities it will be a good thing,' he continues adding that his religion does not come in the way of progress for women.

With Kerala having a large percentage of population bent towards minority politics, Christians, Muslims, etc., he believes that the IUML has worked largely towards the benefit of minorities in the state and has been expanding itself towards other states too like Tamil Nadu and Maharashtra (where the party was quite dominant in the early eighties). In Tamil Nadu, the party has one assembly seat while several of its elected members in the panchayat and corporations. They would like to see themselves reinstated in Mumbai but maintaining proper leadership remains an issue. 'Everyone wants to become a leader,' he says with a smile.

● ● ● ——————— ● ● ●

THE ART OF BEING IN POWER

In this age of coalition politics, managing leaders is an art in itself. Unlike those who prefer to remain at the forefront, there is an equally large number of party workers who run the show from behind the scenes, quietly and anonymously.

While researching for this book, I met many of them; they are not only sought by leaders but also common grassroots workers. Silently toiling away in the background, refusing to share the limelight, these shadow masters, (as I call them) are known by many names, the most common being power brokers. One such prominent power broker, from Mumbai, agrees to speak to me though on conditions on anonymity. Somnath (name changed on request) is a businessman who claims his full-time job is consultancy while doing a 'bit of politics on the side' for his friends who are mainly politicians, 'looking for some advice now and then.' On his speed dial, one can find the mobile numbers of India's leading industrialists and politicians. Somnath begins by saying that 'power broker' is a word created by people who make money. 'I won't call them power brokers but as facilitators without self-interest. Some people want to do something,' he says adding that there are always two people working behind the scenes. The number of power brokers, he claims, is declining day by day.

'In every case, there are people who work behind the scene, especially when there is an alliance government; otherwise, when there is a single-party government what is the need for a broker? Broker means people who come to earn money,' he clarifies further adding that many people are working behind the scene without any expectations. He agrees that it does take some effort to get close to the leader. 'In politics, if you are not close to somebody who is going to make decisions then what is the point? You have to be close to the person, who knows to make the decisions only then things can happen for you. Otherwise, there is nothing. You should be close to someone like that. You need to have a good approach, there is no use if that is not there,' he says. To become close to the leader one needs to convince them and make them trust that one is not their competitor. 'If you are his competitor, then that person will not place his trust in you. The second thing is that you need to assure him that you are not going to misuse the information that he shares with you, and the third most important thing is that you are not going to disclose that information throughout your life and that you will never disclose any talks that may have happened between both of you. If you have these three things in place, only then can you be a genuine facilitator. These three things are important, otherwise, the leader will never place his trust in you,' he states adding that like money, information is equally important to run a political party and leaders spend money on both. 'Foot soldiers today have also become materialistic. When you are in power, the expectations are more to spend money. If you have one person working for you for many years and if you are engaging him to do your work full-time them obviously, he is a full-timer and expects to be paid. It is also natural for him to expect things from the leader or the party. If he has a family, then to take of their needs and expenses he needs to have money. He needs to be reimbursed with a salary.'

Somnath adds that the view from the top is not all that rosy. Leaders, he says who run their parties, find it quite challenging and difficult. 'It isn't easy for them. Ten people come and say 10 things to them, the leader himself has to analyse whom he should listen to and what decision should he take. He will then consult a third party and ask for their clarifications because he has no option. His decision may turn out to be right or wrong—that is a different matter altogether but one thing is sure that if a leader has to make a decision, then he has to rely on inputs from various people, he cannot depend on one person alone.' Internal politics is also a part of politics and leaders too end up managing that. 'If the main leader decides he wants to appoint so and so person at a certain position or give him a ticket, despite the prevailing jealousy, others tend to fall in line.'

One often sees newcomers getting preference over veteran party workers and there is a reason for that. 'There are various instances why this happens. For instance, the leader when he observes that in a particular zilla or an assembly segment, even if his worker who has been working there is unable to either grow the party or win any seats for the party, he thinks that although he is a sincere worker he has limitations. This means that if he continues to stay, then the party will not grow. So, the leader feels he is bound to recruit someone, and in most cases, he gets someone who has already defected from the opposing party.' In some cases, he says, some workers tend to win their seats despite the party they belong to. And the leader prefers to take such workers on board because he sees his party winning and coming to power. 'In many cases, the concept of ideology remains at the side because ultimately it is a numbers game. If you can't win the seat then you can't come to power.'

Leaders do, at times, make mistakes but some leadership qualities are a must if you want to rule.

'One quality you should have is taking everyone along with you, having good oratory skills, good organizational skills and also the ability for political manipulation. The last is a necessity in any case.' Political manipulation, he clarifies, is when the leader has the knowledge and ability of understanding and making use of people as per their positions at that particular time. 'It is the art of balancing and management of people of different personalities while at the same time trying to get your work done from them without upsetting them. It is a 100 per cent stressful job,' he says continuing that apart from all this a bit of honesty too is required. 'The person who has both honesty and integrity is bound to be successful and last but not the least, you should have the ability to win elections. You can't be a leader if you cannot win elections," he sums up.

●●● ——————— ●●●

Dynastic politics is here to stay. We cannot ignore the reality that India will continue to be run by a select group of influential people who are well-versed in the art of politics within their families for generations. Apart from fame and fortune, and connections and accessibility, leaders belonging to dynastic political families have the advantage and the experience of 'being there and done that'. Men and women, born into political families tend to be blessed with everything that a common party worker only desires to have. While some use this opportunity well enough, a majority of them tend to take their good fortune for granted and that is when the problem begins. Rulers born to rule need to equip themselves with not only proper education and experience but also a clear vision of what they want and what they need. When in public life, they need to realize that after all, they are mere custodians of public welfare and that they need to keep their interests aside and focus on the welfare of those less fortunate around them.

Dynastic rulers also need more than that—they need to learn the art of being compassionate to their followers and work towards imbibing in them a sense of empowerment for their existence. Money and power may just be a temporary tonic—because when you uplift an entire society, you live on forever.

REFERENCES

Association for Democratic Reforms. 2020. *Report: Analysis of Funds Collected and Expenditure Incurred by Political Parties during Lok Sabha Elections 2019*. Available at: https://adrindia.org/content/analysis-funds-collected-and-expenditure-incurred-political-parties-during-lok-sabha-0 (accessed on 4 February 2020).

Gokarn, Anjali. 'Communication and People Management'. Women in Politics workshop, SPJIMR.

Greene, Robert. 2010. *The 48 Laws of Power*. New Delhi: Viva Books.

International IDEA. 1998. *Women in Parliament: Beyond Numbers*. Sweden: International IDEA

Karam, Azza, Julie Ballington, Marie-José Protais, Myriam Méndez-Montalvo, and Sakuntala Kadirgamar-Rajasingham. 1998. *Women in Parliament: Beyond Words*. Stockholm: International Idea.

Ministry of Panchayati Raj. 2008. *Elected Women Representatives*. New Delhi: Ministry of Panchayati Raj, Government of India.

Patel, Vibhuti. 2007. 'Gender Budgeting in India'. Available at: https://www.scribd.com/document/240354445/Gender-Budgeting-in-India-by-Vibhuti-Patel (accessed on 15 July).

Sen, Mamta Chitnis. 2019. 'The Evolving Role of Women in Political Parties: A Perspective'. Available at: http://www.mamtasen.com/Evolving%20role%20of%20Women%20in%20Political%20Parties%20by%20Mamta%20Sen.pdf (accessed on 15 July 2020).

Tagore, Rabindranath. 2002. *Rabindra Rachanavali, Talks in China, Lectures Delivered in April and May 1924*. New Delhi: Rupa Publications.

Thakur, Narendra, and Vijay Kranti. 2015. *About RSS—Rashtriya Swayamsewak Sangh*. New Delhi: Vichar Vinimay Prakashan.

The Print. 2019. 'These are India's 34 most powerful political families'. *The Print*, 8 March 2019. Available at: https://theprint.in/politics/these-are-indias-34-most-powerful-political-families/202724/ (accessed on 16 June 2020).

The Tribune. 2019. 'Dynasty Rules, Seven MPs from Political Families'. *The Tribune*, 28 May 2019. Available at:https://www.tribuneindia.com/news/archive/punjab/dynasty-rules-seven-mps-from-political-families-779246 (accessed on 16 June 2020).

ABOUT THE AUTHOR

Mamta Chitnis, artist and writer, has worked with publications such as *Mid-Day*, *Society* and *The Sunday Guardian* where she handled the political beat for Maharashtra. She headed *Dignity Dialogue*, India's foremost magazine exclusively for the 50-plus age group as Executive Editor. She was also the Secretary of the Mumbai Youth Congress from 2007 to 2010.

She has studied painting and ceramics at Sir J. J. School of Art, Mumbai, and was the Hon. Researcher for the art college involved in documenting the history of the institute. During her stint as a student at J. J., she founded Canvas Clan in 2011, a congregation of painters of various age groups and curated two group shows under the banner—*Random Strokes* and *Resurrection Bihar*; the latter was to commemorate centenary celebrations of Bihar state in Mumbai. She was felicitated by the Bihar government for the same.

Mamta was also the Consultant, Media Advocacy, Arts & Crafts and Exhibitions with the Bihar Industrial Area Development Authority (BIADA) and was involved in community outreach programmes for the Bihari Diaspora. She handled Bihar Foundation's art gallery Zierou (which she founded) and organized art exhibitions, workshops and capacity training programmes aimed to promote art and culture in the state.

Women and their rights have been an integral part of her work both in writing and in art. An alumnus of S. P. Jain Institute of Management and Research, Mumbai, where she studied Women Empowerment and Resource Mobilization, Mamta has hosted capacity training workshops for women from political parties as well as from the unorganized sector. She has authored a paper on these experiences titled 'Evolving Role of Women in Political Parties' and since 2012, has been documenting social crises through art. Her recent solo exhibitions on women farmers were at Jehangir Art Gallery and Ministry of External Affairs, Vilnius, Lithuania.

She volunteers with World Citizen Artists—a forum of international artists, musicians and writers, founded in Paris 2013 and was selected to create art for World Humanitarian Day and World Mandela Day. She has been invited by the Mayor of Bressuire in France to showcase her paintings in the city's eleventh-century castle and has exhibited her paintings in various art galleries in India and abroad. Her art has been published in international art journals and anthology such as *Studio to Studio—The Artists' Working Theory and Practice* and *Les Femmes Folles: The Women 2016*.

In 2018 she participated in a month-long art residency in Vilnius, Lithuania hosted by *Sanskritik Mandala*. The works created in the residency were showcased in Vilnius and then later travelled to Berlin, Germany. Her paintings are in private collections in India and countries such as Spain, South Africa, France, Morocco, Denmark, Germany, Lithuania and Belgium.

Since 2015, Mamta has been handling Media Advocacy for Child Rights and You (CRY)—an NGO working for the rights of underprivileged children in India.

Mamta also teaches Journalism and Communications for Development as a guest faculty at St. Xaviers Institute of Communications (XIC) in Mumbai. An avid traveller and writer, she regularly writes for several national and international publications.

Hailed by some as India's steel frame and reviled by others as a relic of the colonial past, the Indian Administrative Service is an enigma for most. In this candid insider account, Naresh Saxena gives the IAS a human face and shares valuable ideas for administrative reform.

Jean Dréze
Honorary Professor, Delhi School of Economics

Loopholes in
IAS Administration

For special
offers on this
and other
books from SAGE,
write to
marketing@sagepub.in

Explore our range at
www.sagepub.in

PAPERBACK
9789353286484

The book addresses two key questions: How madrasas are falsely accused by some politicians of producing radicalized students who pick up arms and indulge in militancy and how some madrasas are trying to find ways to stay relevant in contemporary times by imparting modern knowledge alongside Islamic teachings. The book shall remain relevant for those seeking to reform madrasa education.

Swami Agnivesh
Former Minister of Education, Haryana and social reformer activist

Madrasas at Crossroads

For special offers on this and other books from SAGE, write to marketing@sagepub.in

Explore our range at
www.sagepub.in

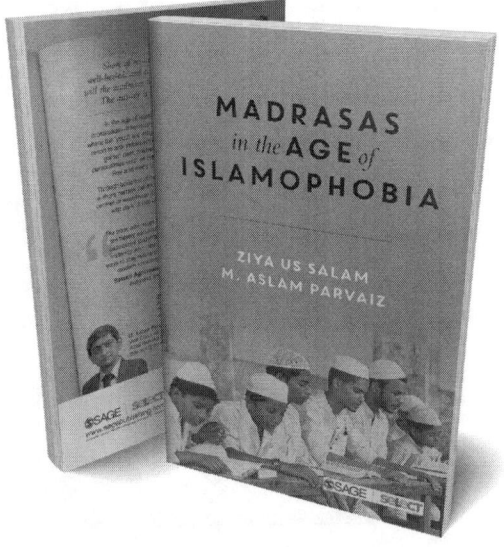

PAPERBACK
9789353289294